Magnetic Leadership

*Expert Consultants, Trainers and Speakers
Share Secrets that Attract People to Your Leadership*

Compiled by Doug Smart

Magnetic Leadership

Managing Editor: Gayle Smart
Editor: Sara Kahan
Proofreader: Laura Johnson
Book Designer: Paula Chance
Copyright ©2003

All rights reserved. No portion of this book may be reproduced in any form without written permission from the publisher.

Disclaimer: This book is a compilation of ideas from numerous experts who have each contributed a chapter. As such, the views expressed in each chapter are those of the authors and not necessarily the views of James & Brookfield Publishers.

For more information, contact:
James & Brookfield Publishers
P.O. Box 768024
Roswell, GA 30076
℃ 770-587-9784

Library of Congress Catalog Number 2003090104

ISBN: 0-9712851-8-7

10 9 8 7 6 5 4 3 2 1

Contents

Be a Magnetic Leader
    Dan Thurmon . . . . .Page 05

Wanted: Leaders with These Five Qualities
    Chet R. Marshall . . . . .Page 19

Leaders and Their Strategies for Success℠
    Natalie Manor . . . . .Page 29

The 1% Leader
    Michael Connor . . . . .Page 43

Leadership is an Art . . . Not a Position
    Bonnie Dean . . . . .Page 53

The End of Dominance:
    The Call for the Multi-Dimensional Leader
    Michelle Cubas. . . . . .Page 67

The Language of Leadership
    Jim Vance . . . . .Page 87

Intuitive Leadership: Transformation and Change
    from the "Insight" Out
    Edie Raether, M.S., CSP . . . . .Page 99

Extreme Trust: The Magnet of EXTREME Leadership™
    Dave Timmons . . . . .Page 113

Ten Strategies for Magnetic Leadership
    Through Your Positive Influence
    Susan B. Wilson, M.B.A., CSP . . . . .Page 125

From the Leader's Message to the Public's Memory
    Karen L. Anderson, M.A., Ed.S. ....*Page 135*

The 3 C's of Life and Leadership
    Candy Whirley ....*Page 147*

Facilitative Leadership:
    Honoring the Minds and Hearts of Others
    Linda Logan-Condon. ....*Page 159*

Links to Leadership
    Michele Matt, CSP and Steve Rutledge ....*Page 173*

Getting to the Finish Line
    Drew Stevens ....*Page 185*

Power Etiquette: Leadership Skills
    That Open Doors Money Cannot
    Dana May Casperson ....*Page 195*

If the Lights Are Out, Write by Candlelight
    Sharon Spano ....*Page 211*

Super Vision Leadership
    Jim Lane ....*Page 221*

Motivating Others to Do What You Want
    Doug Smart, CSP ....*Page 233*

True Leaders Lead Themselves First
    Dr. Bill Newman ....*Page 243*

Resource Listing ....*Page 253*

BE A MAGNETIC LEADER

by Dan Thurmon

Of all the people in your life, who is it that played a role of such significance that you felt changed for the better by knowing them? Maybe it was a family member, a teacher, an employer, or a friend. We have all encountered people who seem to bring the best out of those they touch. Such individuals possess the quality of attraction. They embody a powerful force which pulls others toward their presence, their ideas, and their essence. In short, they are magnetic. What is this power? Why does it affect us? Is it reserved for a select few who were born with the ability, or can all of us, through practice and understanding, develop the power of magnetism? I believe that some individuals possess this skill naturally but that each of us has the capacity to develop and strengthen the "pull" or force of our personal magnetism.

The purpose of this book is to improve your ability to lead others effectively. To me, this means shattering and discarding old and flawed constructs of leadership. One characterization suggests that the person who is the leader is, by definition, the ultimate authority. What he or she says goes, period. The strength of this leader is derived from an ability to push others toward desired results. He cracks the whip. She herds the cattle. I call this style *Assertive Leadership*. Practitioners of this form of leadership use their power, whether it is physical, political, or perceived, to assert their will upon others. Assertive leadership works extremely well in military organizations and is necessary for the chain of command and the execution of orders. When you enlist in the military, you know in advance that following strict commands is part of your job description.

Increasingly, this style of leadership has grown stale and ineffective in the civilian world. People resist being pushed, even if it is with the best intentions. They resent being herded, even if the result is a pasture rich with reward. What, then, is a leader to do? How do you get the best effort from those around you and simultaneously validate and uplift them as individuals? The answer is in *Magnetic Leadership*, and the approach runs counter to traditional theory: Don't push. Pull. Create an attraction that compels others to action, generates excitement, and validates individuals. I would be willing to bet that the people who influenced your life to the greatest degree were those who pulled, not pushed, you to develop. Even in the military, the most successful leaders throughout history have also possessed tremendous magnetism. General George S. Patton's leadership style was one he cultivated and fully exercised. He managed to obtain a supreme effort from his men through the force of his personal magnetism. One reason was that he demanded more of himself than he did of anyone else. Men half his age were hard pressed to keep up with him physically, and he was focused to the extreme on his objectives. Patton was a voracious reader, a student of history, an engineer, and an expert swordsman. His abilities and charisma created a desire among his troops to perform at their highest abilities. As a result, Patton's command was one of the most technically expert and successful during World War II.

Magnetism surrounds us daily. In the physical world, we constantly come in contact with substances that carry magnetic currents. Our planet itself is a huge magnet, charged with a North and South Pole. Understanding magnetism has enabled our ancestors, beginning about 1,000 A.D., to navigate the seas and explore previously uncharted territory. For centuries, people have benefited from using magnets for health benefits, including the increase of circulation in the human body. With each new discovery we confirm that human beings are not separate from our natural world. We are a part of it. Therefore, if we seek to learn a little about the science of attraction, we will actually learn more about ourselves.

Hypothesis

Magnets, or substances that have magnetic properties, naturally attract iron and other items like themselves. If we understand how this is accomplished and the universal laws that enable this attraction, then we can utilize this same power to more effectively draw others to our ideas and leadership initiatives.

Magnets attract, but they also have the simultaneous capacity to repel. A magnet contains both a North and South Pole. Even when we attempt to remove one of the poles by breaking or cutting a magnet, new poles are instantly created at the broken ends to restore the wonderfully balanced state of magnetism.

Human beings also experience the dynamics of having two "poles," and we remain in balance through our ability to see both sides of any issue. We have an innate ability to experience opposite emotions, opinions, and courses of action at the same time. At first it seems like a contradiction, but within each of us two completely different perspectives exist simultaneously. One example is the proud parent who experiences tremendous happiness at his daughter's graduation ceremony while also feeling sadness that she is moving on to the next phase of life. Or consider the debater who must understand and be able to articulate both sides of an issue in order to fully prepare to promote her position. By seeing a situation from differing perspectives, or poles, simultaneously, we are able to reason, use judgment, and make informed choices about how we process the world around us.

The choices we make create our reality. What we choose to believe determines how we feel, what we think, what we do, and how we interact with others. When we invest ourselves in a particular pattern of thinking or acting, we begin to attract into our lives people, experiences, and information that support our investment. For example, remember a time when you became interested in an idea or an experience for the first time? Perhaps you just got a new car. Suddenly, you seem to notice the same make of automobile everywhere you look! Or you develop an interest in a new hobby and mysteriously begin to meet other people who share your interest. That is your magnetism at work.

Magnetic Fields

I asked my three-year-old son, Eddie, what he knew about magnets. He replied, "Those are the things we put on the refrigerator." Good answer. But, let's look a bit further. How, exactly, does it stay there on the refrigerator?

A magnet will attract a piece of iron even though the two are not in direct contact. This attraction that takes place at a distance is said to be due to the magnetic field, or field of force, around the magnet. The stronger the force, or field strength, of the magnet, the greater the reach of its attraction.

"Extra" Electrons

A magnetic attraction is created when there is an imbalance in the number of electrons between two substances. A magnetic needle is lacking in electrons. The magnetic force of our planet's North Pole contains an abundance of electrons. Seeking completion, the needle responds without fail, aligning itself with the source of what it needs most.

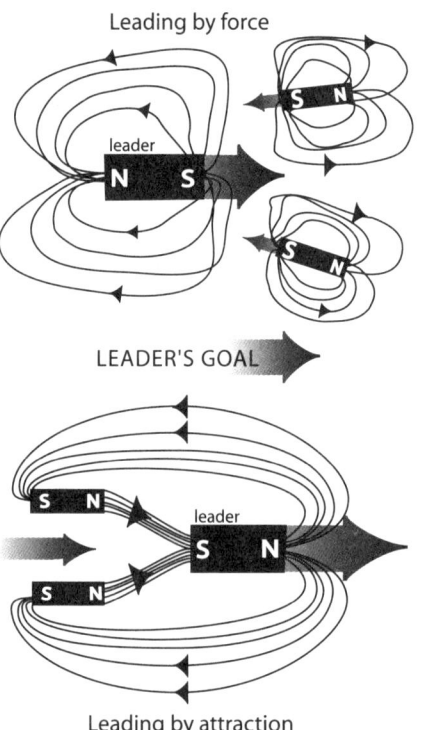

Try this yourself. A needle can be made magnetic by rubbing it with silk. The silk has the effect of removing electrons from the needle. Then, place the needle on a leaf and float it in water. You will have made your very own compass.

What do people need most? If you can answer that question and then supply what is needed, you will increase the strength of your magnetic field, which, in turn, will draw people toward you and expand your capacity to lead.

As leaders, if we can provide an abundance of what is lacking, others will be drawn to us without much additional effort. In other words, we must focus our efforts first on creating a compelling and substantive foundation for our attraction, our magnetic field. We must work on ourselves and ensure that we are in balance with the qualities we wish to attract. What are people lacking? As I work with organizations and individuals across the nation, I repeatedly encounter many of the same answers, regardless of the industry involved. People feel a lack of validation for who they are and what they do.

Validation

In 1929, at the age of eighteen, a small Albanian girl left the security and comfort of home to follow a calling from God to minister to the needs of the poorest of the poor in India. Still feeling a desire to do more, each year she asked permission from Rome to leave her convent and work among the sick and dying on the streets of Calcutta. It was twenty years before her request was granted. Then, she began to lift people from the street and shelter them, clean them, feed them, smile at them, touch them, and, especially, love them. Her tireless efforts gave men and women dignity and respect, often at the very end of their lives. As a result, Mother Teresa led a life of awe-inspiring magnetism. She validated each individual she touched. She made each person feel important, special, and loved. Her magnetism drew thousands to join her order, the Missionaries of Charity, and further this work across the world. In more than forty years, the Missionaries of Charity have lifted more than 54,000 people from the streets of Calcutta, and more than 23,000 have died at the Home for the Dying in Calcutta with dignity, respect, and validation.

Every one of us needs validation: We feel the need to be understood, acknowledged, and supported for who we are and what we think. We want to be heard. This doesn't necessarily mean that we want everyone to agree with us all of the time. But we do want others to take us and our ideas seriously. Even someone who disagrees with you can provide validation by respecting your position and entering into discussion. As a leader, you can implement five skills to insure that you are providing validation to those within the scope of your influence. Develop these skills in abundance, and you will create a powerful pull, a force that attracts people to you and affects them in a positive and meaningful way.

1. Practice active listening

This skill is paramount to developing rich connections and empathy during our communications. To exhibit this skill, we must be engaged and actively participating in the listening process. We are focused intently on our counterpart. As this person speaks, we listen with purpose, making every effort to understand what we hear. When in doubt about something, ask questions to clarify your understanding. When the other person finishes, restate what you have heard in your own words to demonstrate that you have listened and received the message. Interpret what you have heard and contribute to the idea with your own thoughts and information, but only after you have acknowledged, or validated, the other person's perspective.

2. Supply positive reinforcement

The most effective form of behavior modification, whether you are training animals, raising children, or leading a team of employees, is positive reinforcement. When you recognize and reward someone, you instantly validate that person. When you conduct your recognition publicly, rewarding and praising someone in front of his peers, the results are even more extraordinary. Praise and confirmation that we have done a good job is a motivator that, for many people, is more personally rewarding than their paycheck. If you are in a position of leadership, you must be attuned to what isn't working and what needs improvement in order to take corrective action. But effective and *magnetic* leaders are also always in the process of looking for positive actions and qualities. When you do spot them, take action immediately and offer praise, thanks, and acknowledgement. Do this publicly, when possible. You'll be amazed at the results. The rewarded individual will be energized and uplifted, and others will respond and adapt their efforts to seek the same recognition.

3. Celebrate differences

Magnetic leaders understand that the strength of any group of individuals resides in the diversity and combined experience of the group. The ideal environment for productivity enhances and celebrates the uniqueness of individuals while maintaining focus on a common, compelling goal. This leader conveys the vision of what is possible and generates excitement. Then, he or she looks to the team and invites diverse and creative approaches to move forward toward the goal. The result is an environment where everyone feels involved and validated for his or her contribution. Acknowledge the most positive qualities of each individual. Reflect those qualities back to each person through your own words and actions. When you dismiss an idea or choose a path that varies from what your people have suggested, make your case and present it in a way that continues to validate the contributions of the team. For example, you might say, "Bob, you are really on to something here, but let's take that idea a step further," or "That's what I thought at first, Beth, but then I considered this angle." Statements such as these are encouraging and validating and also offer direction.

4. Focus on mission

In addition to being validated personally, people need to feel that their life and actions have purpose and meaning. We have all searched for direction at various times in our lives. The underlying question is "Why does this matter?" We seek a life that has a reason, a meaningful mission to fulfill. Effective leaders create a magnetic attraction to their mission. The goal takes on a life of its own, providing a compelling, noble, and exciting purpose for action. One of the best examples of magnetic leadership in our nation was born when John F. Kennedy announced a ten-year mission to put an American on the moon and return him safely to Earth. Here was a goal that seemed so incredible and exciting that our country was magnetically attracted to it, and hundreds of thousands of individuals became focused and challenged to put forth their best efforts to make it happen. Technologies were created and discoveries took place at a feverish pace, all because we were focused on a mission. The mission was compelling and the purpose was important because we were working not only to achieve the goal, but also to prove ourselves and our superiority over our biggest rival at that time, the Soviet Union. The result was a successful mission, Apollo 11, culminating on July 20, 1969, when Neil Armstrong took "one small step for man; one giant leap for Mankind." This continues to stand as one of America's proudest moments.

5. Provide alternatives

Have you ever felt that you had no control? The feeling of having no control is very much like helplessness. When we have no control, we are at the mercy of our environment. It is extremely uncomfortable and frustrating, and people usually react to this situation by withdrawing or becoming angry. We want to have at least some control of the outcome or at least the process for reaching the outcome. Control relates to the resources we possess and the alternatives that we have before us. If your leadership style dictates a rigid plan of action without input from your people, your plan may compel others to action, but it might not be the actions you intended. In fact, they are likely to rebel against your leadership. Remember the French Revolution? The leadership of France, Louis XVI and Marie Antoinette, offered no input or alternatives for their citizens, so, the citizens rebelled and even cut off their leader's heads. On the other hand, if you can create choices and provide alternatives within the plan, you enlist the best ideas and efforts of your team and enable positive action. We also provide alternatives by offering opportunities for continued growth and education. The most successful organizations today offer their employees the freedom of choice in developing a career path. Additionally, these companies provide the resources, education, training, and guidance needed to pursue that path with confidence.

Address the Person, not the Role

People want to feel special. It doesn't take much extra effort to make them feel that way, either. In order to make someone feel special during your interactions, simply follow this guiding principle: Address the person, not the role. Connect with the actual human being in front of you, and don't resort to relating to that person according to his or her prescribed role, whatever it may be.

I travel nearly every week to deliver speeches around the country. As you can imagine, the hardest part of traveling is being away from my family. During one particular trip, about a year ago, I had been gone for five days and really missed my wife, Sheilia, and son, Eddie, who was then two years old. So, when I arrived in Atlanta, instead of driving home, I headed straight to a friend's house, where I knew they were visiting. Once I got there, I went around to the back yard, where I knew that Eddie and his friend, Ben, would be on the playground. I was halfway across the yard when Eddie looked up and saw me coming. His face lit up, he turned to Ben and enthusiastically exclaimed, "Look! That's my friend, Daddy!" That's my *friend*, Daddy. What a powerful moment. He made me feel so special, validated, and uplifted in the blink of an eye. And the reason it was so powerful and meaningful is that he didn't address me in the role I was playing in his life, by saying "That's my Dad," or "Hey, look, Ben, it's this guy I know, and his job is being my Dad." No. He addressed me as a person and as a friend.

If you connect with the people in your life as people, or better yet, friends, then you can create the same powerful force that Eddie did that day. You can expand your magnetic field immensely.

What are some of the roles we encounter? There's the gas station attendant, the bank teller, the grocery store clerk, the janitor, the boss, the wife, the husband, the kids, and the employees, to name a few. And behind every role is a person who needs validation. One simple thing I do to accomplish this is to use the person's name. If someone is wearing a name tag, then I will address that person by name, even if we are complete strangers. After all, he or she is wearing a name tag. Why is that? Well, maybe it is so we can read the name and use it! You'll be amazed at the power of this one simple suggestion. People love to hear the sound of their own name. You could also reach out to people by asking questions, offering assistance, or just looking at a situation from their perspective. People will respond to you and go out of their way to help you if you will address the person, not the role.

Magnetic Encounters

It is said that opposites attract and like objects repel. This statement is true when applied to the magnetic poles. North attracts south and repels north every time. We have all heard the saying, "opposites attract." Is it then true that opposite individuals, those who possess very different qualities, attract one another and similar individuals, those who share similar qualities, repel? No. Remember that every individual, like every magnetic field, contains two poles, oppositely charged, simultaneously. This means that you have the capability of connecting with anyone, as long as you achieve the proper relationship of your poles to their poles.

When faced with a confrontational encounter or when you just can't seem to connect with someone, how can you overcome the obstacle? Change your magnetic field. Change your orientation, or your positioning, relative to the other person. If you are repelling one another, it means that aspects of your respective characters are lined up at the wrong poles. You are projecting toward one another "too much of the same thing." In this exchange, there is not a mutual sharing of what the other side requires.

The ultimate goal is to seek completion. What does the person you are connecting with need to become more complete? Provide resources and emotional support to energize people in a way that propels them forward and brings out all their strengths and abilities. When you orient yourself to give an abundance of what they need, then you become magnetic. You create an attraction that will propel them forward. That is magnetic leadership.

A magnetic current between two people may start out small and grow through interaction and an exchange of dialogue. The most productive strategy is to find some common area of agreement, a first step in the process of validation. This is one reason why people talk about the weather. I live in Atlanta, Georgia, where the summer temperature can be brutally hot and humid. Everyone experiences it together. So, when one person encounters another and proudly exclaims, "Sure is hot today," it's not exactly a new piece of information. It's a statement of the obvious. It's an opportunity for the other person to offer validation, saying, "Sure is." If you can find one area of agreement, no matter how small or trivial, it will generate an emotional connection and provide momentum on which your relationship can grow. So, always be in the process of trying to find areas of agreement.

Enhanced Magnetism

The strength of a magnetic field is not constant. As we look to science, there are other factors that can contribute to or take away from the strength of attraction. Let's quickly consider three steps you can take to boost your magnetism in a positive way.

1. Add energy

A magnet excited by electric current (energy) can lift many times its own weight. The first electromagnet was constructed in 1825 by William Sturgeon and successfully lifted objects twenty times its weight. What does this mean to you? It means if you will "get excited," or become energized, the power of your magnetic field will increase dramatically. This is the reason why sports teams have cheerleaders. When the fans become excited and add their energy in support of the team, quite often the result is a more motivated and resourceful team. Leaders also play the role of cheerleader. But you can give away energy only if you have it in abundance. What about the times when you feel like you could use a cheerleader of your own? We can add energy to our lives through proper nutrition and regular exercise. We can interact with energetic people and maintain a constant flow of inspirational and educational experiences in our life. We can also schedule activities that will generate energy and keep momentum moving forward. For example, schedule meetings in a location outside the office that provides stimulation, such as a park or outdoor café. Or, shorten the length of your meetings to sharpen the focus of participants and increase the pace and exchange of energy.

2. Adjust your temperature

Temperature also affects magnetic strength. One experiment demonstrated that magnetized iron lost its magnetism when heated to a bright red heat and regained it when it cooled back to room temperature.

What's the lesson for us? Watch your temperature. When we "get hot" by becoming angry or losing our temper, we no longer maintain a magnetic attraction. We don't draw people toward us. We push them away. When we are angry, or "hot," we are without the resources for leading others. Fortunately, this condition is temporary. If we will "cool back down" and regain control of our emotions and resources, we will also regain our magnetism. Then, we can once again serve others and provide what they need to move forward.

3. Reduce stress

The magnetic properties of many materials are so sensitive to the application of stress that stress may be ranked with field strength and temperature as a primary factor affecting magnetic change. As the amount of stress on a magnet increases, its magnetic ability drops considerably. Stress impedes the magnet process and significantly reduces the force of attraction. Do you think that this scientific fact also applies to human beings? I certainly do. People, like magnetic materials, are extremely sensitive to the effects of stress. Stress sets off an alarm reaction in the body, initiating a "fight or flight" mechanism. Adrenalin flows through the body. Heart rate and pulse begin to rise. The immune system functions less effectively, making a person more susceptible to illness. Mental effects of sustained stress include depression, anxiety, and irritability. These conditions do not make a leader more empowered or resourceful. Quite the opposite is true. When you experience stress, your magnetic field is reduced. Your energy is depleted. You are less effective at attracting and persuading others. When you are stressed, people do not want what you have. Therefore, if you want to be a magnetic leader, it is mandatory that you maintain control of your life and your level of stress. Some stress is unavoidable. But you must learn how to manage and diffuse the stress that comes into your life. Take breaks to incorporate fun and activity into your day. Step back from a stressful situation, and don't make important decisions while experiencing stress. Instead, wait until you can process information with a clear mind and all of your resources.

Conclusion

Are you magnetic? Yes, absolutely. What elements are you currently attracting and what is the strength of your magnetic field? That is entirely up to you. The principles outlined in this chapter, inspired by scientific observation, will help you manage and increase your power of influence only if you take action. Put these ideas into action, and you are sure to be a master of Magnetic Leadership and an inspiration to the many people you touch. You will play a role of such significance that people will feel changed for the better for knowing you and following your example.

About Dan Thurmon

*D*an Thurmon *speaks to businesses and organizations teaching people to transcend the ordinary, find balance, and achieve breakthroughs in all areas of life. Originally from Chicago, he attended the University of Georgia, graduating with a degree in Marketing in 1990. Dan has also studied business management, music, theater, dance, gymnastics and aviation. He is a member of the National Speakers Association and International Federation of Speakers. He presently lives in Atlanta, GA, with his wife, Sheilia and children, Eddie and Maggie. Dan has worked with hundreds of organizations including IBM, The Coca-Cola Company, Shaw Industries, AT&T and Kimberly Clark Corporation. He has also appeared on national television, including* The Late Show with David Letterman. *A multi-talented communicator, Dan serves as a valuable asset to organizations as they put ideas into action.*

Contact Information:
Dan Thurmon
Motivation Works, Inc.
1905 Scenic Highway, Suite 640-214
Snellville, GA 30078
Phone: (770) 982-2664
E-mail: dan@danthurmon.com
Website: www.danthurmon.com

Wanted: Leaders with These Five Qualities

by Chet R. Marshall

"Please write down the names of three individuals whom you come in contact with that you recognize as true leaders. People that you respect because of their ability to effectively lead," I say to my audiences as I prepare to talk about leadership. Just three names! In the twenty- plus years I've been talking about leadership, it still amazes me how difficult a task this seems to be for audiences. Just three names!

The second task I give to audiences is usually a little easier. "Write down the qualities these leaders have that cause you to recognize them as leaders." The writing down of qualities seems to flow fairly freely. We all seem to recognize the traits, characteristics, and qualities of leaders; it's the leader themselves who are difficult to identify.

Once the audience has completed these tasks, we have a popcorn session. In a popcorn session, one audience member after another calls out a quality he or she has written down. I furiously write them on a flipchart page, not leaving any blank spaces on that single page. The page is full of qualities it takes to be an effective leader, and when I look at that long list, it makes me tired just thinking about what it takes to be an effective leader. I then ask the audience of leaders and wanna-be leaders, "How do you measure up?"

In this exercise, which I've been doing more than twenty years, there are five qualities that are mentioned every single time, without fail. Usually they are among the first few called out during the popcorn session.

Indeed, there are many requirements and qualities necessary to be effective in a leadership role or position. But I believe these five qualities are an absolute must to create "Magnetic Leadership." These five qualities are certainly the core principles of leadership. They provide a solid foundation on which to construct a leadership character of strength and magnetism. These five qualities are the litmus test for wanna-be leaders. Without these, you continue to be a follower at best. That's why I've titled this chapter "Wanted, Leaders with These Five Qualities."

Let me share a story with you I call the "Giannini Phenomenon," which I believe epitomizes these five qualities as well. The Bank of America had just celebrated an outstanding year, and many of those responsible were at a company meeting. During a question-and-answer session, one of the bank officers observed, "What we need at Bank of America is one more Giannini." Giannini was the founder of the Bank of Italy, which later became the Bank of America.

When asked, "Why do we need one more Giannini?" the officer replied, "When Giannini was here you knew it. If you did a good job, he told you. If you didn't, he let you know. Giannini was visible and accessible. He was capable of relating to other human beings face-to-face and person-to-person. He was able to communicate: "I know, I understand, I am concerned, and I care."

In defining leadership, this banker was right on target. Leaders are people, who are indeed visible and accessible. They place a high premium on face-to-face, honest interaction. Others know they are truly concerned, knowledgeable, and caring.

In most organizations, it is apparent that, if there is a shortage of anything today, it is indeed a shortage of Gianninis. Individuals in command positions and leadership roles who are, by design, visible and accessible and who can continually communicate to others, "I know, I understand, I am concerned, and I care."

Do you know anyone like that? We need to make the distinction that leadership in the 21st century is performance, not position. Leadership does not happen from the 52nd floor of a headquarters building. Leaders stay in touch — with social, political, technological, and economic trends and, most importantly, with those who are following and also being empowered to lead.

Keeping the "Giannini Phenomenon" in mind, let's look at the five qualities leaders must have to be effective in the 21st century, as recognized by audiences all across the nation

1. Trust — To trust and be trusted is an essential quality for every effective leader.

In the early seventies, I assumed a new position as director of finance with a county school system. The department consisted of three employees, all of them with long tenure. One employee in particular had been there over twenty years and had worked with the superintendent when the entire central office staff consisted of two, she and the superintendent.

Within a six-month period of time she had tested my diplomacy as well as my Christianity with many challenges. There was one issue in particular she was very emphatic about, stating, *"I'm not doing it, you will."* I diplomatically reminded her of her areas of responsibility and that this duty fell in her area. Her response, *"Well, I'll just talk to the superintendent."* My response, *"I believe that's a good idea; let's do it now."*

Much to her surprise, when we walked into the superintendent's office, I simply informed him she had something she wanted to talk to him about. As she stumbled over her words and started to explain the issue, he realized the direction she was going and stopped her in mid-explanation.

He said, *"You and I go a long way back, you've been an exemplary employee, but you need to understand one thing right now, you work for Mr. Marshall and he knows what your responsibility is. If you don't feel you can handle that, maybe you need to find something else to do."*

The superintendent, being the leader he was, gave me confidence I could trust him and his support. At the same time, he demonstrated he trusted me to lead and handle the responsibilities of the department. The employee was exemplary, and we went on to have a great relationship.

2. Communication — An effective leader is a good communicator not because of what he says, but what he hears. Giannini's ability to communicate, "I know, I understand, I am concerned, and I care" demonstrates a leader who listens.

Listen! The ears of a good communicator get more exercise than their mouth. Dean Rusk, former Secretary of State, said, *"One of the best ways to persuade others is with your ears."*

"Thanks, you've really helped me," my friend said as he got up to leave. I sat in my chair and pondered that statement for a while before making a move, realizing I had barely said anything at all. Later that day, my friend called me to say I had been the fourth person he had attempted to talk to, but I was the only one who had listened. Having the opportunity to talk through what he was dealing with was exactly what he needed. As he talked through it, he was able to formulate his action plan.

A great leader is not someone who has to be listened to but someone who has the innate ability to listen. It's difficult to have your ears and mouth engaged at the same time.

How many times have you heard someone say, *"Oh, they talk real well, they just never listen"*?

3. Caring — Effective leadership involves taking care of people in many ways. Giannini in his communicating, "and I care," demonstrates this leadership quality. When the bank officer said, "When you did a good job, he told you; if you didn't, he let you know," Giannini was letting people know he truly cared. The other caring aspect I gleaned from the "Giannini Phenomenon" was that he didn't just care about job performance but also about the individual.

"Mr. Marshall, can you come with me a moment?" she said. I got up from my desk and followed her to the back stairs, where she showed me a stair tread that was loose and frayed. She was concerned one of the employees would catch a heel and fall.

Some three hours later I was coming out of the men's room and overheard this same employee telling another employee, *"He's already fixed it. He really cares about us."*

Praise is also very important in taking care of people. *People work for love and money; which do you have the most of? Are you willing to spend a little love?*

Leaders should get up in the morning thanking people, at noon thanking more people, and, before they leave at night, thank even more people.

Dr. Sheila Murray Bethel, author, speaker and my mentor was the first person I heard say, *"People don't care how much you know until they know how much you care."*

4. Visibility and Approachability — An effective leader must have special attributes, but personal attention makes people feel special. The story of Giannini certainly shows us the visibility and approachability of this effective leader. It's difficult to follow someone you never see or have no communication with. Morale and productivity are always raised to higher levels when the leader is available and easy to talk to.

In the mid-nineties I decided to semi-retire to pursue a real passion in my life, professional speaking. I was maintaining two homes in two different cities and therefore was not as available as I had been in the past. I left the reins and leadership of my company in the hands of a very capable individual. He did an excellent job.

It was a difficult transition for the employees, however, simply because our leadership styles were different. When I was there, I would always go to every person in our company and touch their lives in some way, sometimes by asking questions, sometimes by making statements or telling a story. I always maintained an open-door policy, and they knew they could come and talk with me about anything at anytime. I always made time for them and demonstrated they were a priority in my life and business.

Leaders should thrive on being visible and approachable. We've all seen people in important positions who were leaders by position only, not by performance. In part, they attempt to lead by intimidation, they strut instead of walk, inhale but never exhale, frown instead of smile, and love every minute of it.

Effective leaders are true leaders by performance and demonstrate to others their visibility, approachability, and accessibility.

5. Integrity — An effective leader exudes integrity that eliminates any questions to the contrary. The integrity of Giannini is definitely revealed in what the bank officer had to say about him. It leaves no question.

There is no pillow as soft as a clear conscience. Too many people sit in board or committee meetings trying to find a way to do something wrong in the right way. It can't be done.

"But if we put this procedure code on this procedure, we can get paid for it."

"But that's not exactly the procedure being done."

"But, but, but . . ."

There is no right way to do a wrong thing.

There was a skit presented for children at our church one Sunday morning that I have never forgotten. The scene was a living room where the father was folding towels from a basket. While doing this task, he was reprimanding one of the children who had lied about taking a cookie from a batch just out of the oven.

The father was lecturing on the importance of not lying or stealing and how God was not pleased with those actions. He had made his point clear and as the child was walking from the room, the next towel Dad pulled from the basket had a Holiday Inn logo on it. The father paused when he saw it and the message sank in.

A few years ago I sat down with a group of people in the speaking profession who were mentors and people I admired. We were having an ad hoc brainstorm session. I mentioned that I was thinking about putting together a keynote presentation on "Integrity." Very quickly and in no uncertain terms I was told that it was a bad idea. It wouldn't sell. People are not interested in that topic. Leaders of organizations don't even want a hint of the thought that they may have integrity issues to deal with. It's very negative; people want more positive material. Nothing that questions integrity would be received well at all.

Recently, our business world, the political world, and unfortunately, our religious world have been deluged with integrity issues. Corporations, associations, and organizations are now clamoring for sessions, seminars, and keynote presentations on integrity and character.

I heard recently, "Integrity is what you do when no one else is watching." I say integrity is a quality without which you can't even think about being a leader. There's no such thing as a leader without integrity. Integrity is usually the first quality mentioned from the audience during our popcorn session. What does that tell you?

Those are the five qualities you must possess to be an effective leader according to my nationwide audiences responses. On a scale of 1 to 10 how would you rate yourself as a leader?

Effective Leadership Quality	SCALE 1-10 (10 highest)
Integrity (If integrity is not a 10, there's no need to go any further, you don't have what it takes to be an effective leader)	_____
Visibility and Approachability	_____
Caring	_____
Communication	_____
Trust	_____

Do you have some room to improve, have some work to do? Are you an effective leader possessing and demonstrating these five qualities and much more? Do you exemplify the "Giannini Phenomenon"?

Early in my life, one of my elementary teachers wrote in my report card, "Chester is a leader in class." It meant little to me at the time, but as I continued through school the label stuck, whether it was in academics, sports, church, or everyday life. Leadership is an awesome responsibility.

Peter Drucker's definition of leadership is the definition I've been using for years. My goal is to help elevate people and leaders to the next level. I believe Drucker's definition speaks to that elevation process as he defines leadership this way:

Leadership is . . .
- *Lifting a person's vision to higher sights*
- *Raising a person's performance to a higher standard*
- *Building a personality beyond its normal limitations.*

The rapidly changing world we live in makes effective leadership more critical than it has ever been. The five qualities in this chapter are not only desirable but are a must in order for leaders to act effectively.

WANTED: LEADERS WITH THESE FIVE QUALITIES is a product of audiences all across the nation giving priority to the qualities of Trust, Communication, Caring, Visibility and Approachability and the absolute must of Integrity. These five qualities are the springboard to effective leadership and enable you to go to the next level. Do you qualify? Are you a Giannini? If you do, and you are, we want you!

ABOUT
CHET R. MARSHALL

*C*het Marshall is a rare find in the arena of professional speaking. His rich background in the corporate world includes several years in healthcare administration, finance, manufacturing, retail and entrepreneurship. An experienced CEO in several industries, Chet is an expert on leadership and management. He is an author and co-author of several books on leadership, success and change. Chet's warm and refreshing sense of humor sparks all of his presentations. He is active in the Fellowship of Christian Athletes and works with youth, encouraging their growth and success. If you're looking for powerful, humorous and meaningful all wrapped up in one creative package, Chet is the right speaker for your event.

Contact Information:
Chet R. Marshall
Elevation Express
130 Summit Ridge
Hurricane, WV 25526
Phone: (304) 545-5100
Fax: (304) 757-5651
E-mail: chetinwv@aol.com

LEADERS AND THEIR STRATEGIES FOR SUCCESS[sm]
From Completing Tasks to High-Visibility Leadership

by Natalie Manor

Patricia is the vice president of operations in a small corporation (of fewer than 20 employees) in Boston. The company has been in operation since 1989 and is owned by Patricia and her partner, Tim. The company is not doing well, revenues are slipping, and the employees are on the verge of belligerence with clients, prospects, and each other.

Patricia and Tim have refinanced their company twice to cover weekly payroll and overhead expenses. They are barely keeping their heads above the proverbial water line.

What is fascinating is that Patricia and Tim both are experts in their chosen industry markets and have demonstrated brilliant consulting with individual customers in the past.

So what is their problem?

Their industry has changed over the last five years. They spend most of their days managing endless paper tasks, continue to supervise their employees like a prosperous company, and have not learned the art of planning and strategizing. They are Hope Leaders[sm].

Example 1 — So What Is a Hope Leader[sm]?

- I hope we get it done in time.
- I hope they pay the bill on time.
- I hope the project is given to us.

- I hope the employees understand we need them to work faster.
- I hope that business picks up soon.

Next, there is Marie. She creates confusion and chaos. As president, owner and CEO of a small corporation, her employees literally hate when she comes in the door and says, "Wait until you hear this. I've got a great idea!" After 16 years of great seat-of-the-pants ideas, four facility-wide rehabs in the last two years, six new products this year and 40 percent rejection and errors of product, they are justified in hiding. Each time a product was developed, the employees worked without a plan, budget or timeline.

Marie cannot understand why her employees and managers run for the hills, and in some cases, just plain resist new ideas — no matter how fun, innovative, or high revenue the possibilities are. She does not understand that what is fun and innovative to her is unclear and difficult for them.

Marie is an Implied Communication[sm] leader.

Example 2 — What is an Implied Communication Leader[sm]?

When communication is not clear, we can ask questions about missing information. When communication is implied, it relies on past ways of doing things, such as "remember how; do it the way we always do it; make sure it works like the last one." We imply that whom we are communicating with understands what we are referencing for information. So we wonder instead of know. Asking people to make decisions and judgments without good, clear information creates questions and statements like these:

- Wonder if this fits the current production schedule?
- I bet this job will be just like the one last Tuesday.
- Sure, we can use the old stuff in the production room to make the new product.
- All the clients will adore this idea.
- Wonder how much we should charge for it?

Example 3 — The Hurt Feelings Leader[sm]?

The Hurt Feelings Leader[sm] takes every piece of feedback personally. Not only do they make business issues a personal issue, they make it almost impossible to communicate with them because they create emotional situations out of everyday business situations.

This is the "Hurt Feelings" Leader.sm Because such leaders cannot deal with the facts at hand, people avoid them. These leaders personalize every issue as a failure, a hurt or an affront.

The Hurt Feelings Leadersm can often be the most difficult to deal with. In order to help them change, you need to spend time helping them to understand what their contribution to a given situation really is.

LEADERSHIP — Start with the Strengths

For the past seventeen years, I've had the privilege of dealing with leaders at all levels of business. All of these successful leaders, male or female, have had traits and characteristics that easily identify them as leaders.

Enthusiastic — their whole body gets involved

Caring — you can feel that they care

Trusting — they take care of the needs of others

Curious — they want to know what makes something work

Risk Taking — take calculated risks to help move the idea ahead and make it successful — willing to be wrong

Intuitive — they sense what others can't or won't see

Innovative — willing to try something new

Visionary — passionate for an idea or a possibility

Strategic — willing to think, plan, and do the the research to make an idea successful

Communicative — find the information or people to do the job, listen to their ideas, communicate the strategies and plan fully the implementation of the project

Practical — have a deep respect for the budget, numbers, and what money can do for the vision

Disciplined — do what needs to be done in a timely manner.

Emerging leaders become successful by putting each piece of leadership into place as they grow. And as they grow themselves into the role of leader, they find that each trait is solidly linked to the others.

The Hope Leader sm *:*
Will be handled and instead proactively plan for them to be handled.

When we finally admit that we have little or no time to manage an issue and it won't go away, we need to find out what is to be done with the issue(s).

Pat and Tim are dealing with employees who are working within a 10-year-old way of doing business. They have:
- billing issues
- time management issues
- project management problems
- unmet employee expectations
- immediate business and revenue crises

As a first step in helping them understand their frustrations with their long-term business problems (that were not going away by *hoping* them away), I asked them to complete the DISC (Dominance, Influencing, Steadiness, and Compliance) Assessment by TTI, Ltd.

The DISC is a marvelous tool for any level of management or key employee because it identifies needs and highlights improvement without guesswork.

The DISC Assessment states:

"Behavioral research suggests that the most effective people are those who understand themselves, both their strengths and weaknesses, so they can develop strategies to meet the demands of their environment.

A person's behavior is a necessary and integral part of who they are. In other words, much of our behavior comes from 'nature' (inherent), and much come from 'nurture' (our upbringing). It is the universal language of 'how we act' or our observable human behavior.

In the DISC report, we are measuring four dimensions of moral behavior. These include:
- *how you respond to problems and challengers*
- *how you influence others to your point of view*
- *how you respond to the pace of the environment*
- *how you respond to rules and procedures set by others*

This report analyzes behavioral style; that is, a person's manner of doing things."

For Pat and Tim, the DISC immediately revealed the areas in which they were hoping their employees would improve. Pat and Tim discovered that they were communicating in incomplete ways that did not accomplish what was needed.

Pat and Tim were immediately able to use their time more wisely in order to lead their small corporation to improved effectiveness and higher revenues. How was this result achieved?

1. Pat began to have a one-hour one-on-one session every week at a regularly scheduled time with her key contributors and thus increase the communication and clarity the business methods needed to increase revenues.
2. The key employees felt listened to and acknowledged by the new attention to their requests, input, suggestions, and concerns. Consequently, they more easily embraced the changes needed to increase effectiveness and revenues.
3. Marketing and relationship building with buyers and clients was designed so that all employees had input on how to deal effectively with their client population and prospects.
4. Pat and Tim began to state their requests and business needs in clear, concise ways. Many old policies were reviewed and either revised based on employee input or tossed out completely because they were outdated.
5. A key employee who was not effective was evaluated based on company needs and reassigned to a different position where he could be more effective (and much happier).

Pat and Tim improved their personal leadership traits and their company's leadership traits by taking the time to stop hoping for change and effectiveness and creating it with action. They involved their key success components — their employees — in redesigning a very effective, revenue-producing company.

Leadership Traits Increased by: Caring, Doing the Numbers, Listening, Communicating, and Being Strategic

As we begin to dissect Marie's lack of leadership traits, the Implied Communication Leader,[sm] we can clearly see where she has tremendous opportunity to move her established business into an effective and revenue producing organization.

So what do we know about Marie and her business?

1. She has been in business for 16 years. That is an indicator of something being done correctly. In 16 years she would have taken in the current business slump, two stock market plunges, and the rough recession ten years ago.
2. The production facility has gone through four complete rehabs in the past two years indicating that she is generating some serious revenues. Rehabs in any facility are costly from a hardware point of view because of the disruption of production.
3. The company turned out six new products in the past year. That certainly indicates that her employee population can plan, react, build, and ship at a phenomenal rate.

So what is the problem with Marie and her company?

Employees' hiding from her product announcements indicates some very serious flaws in the communication link of the organization. It also indicates that they might have the strategic mission of "ready, fire, aim." Unclear actions can cause confusion, lost time, lost revenues, insecurity with employees, and mistrust with the customers.

The enormous growth opening here for Marie and her company involves planning, communication, industry research, strategic development, and rollout.

The outcome of the company-wide meeting was eye opening for Marie and the rest of the employees. They came up with some easy fixes, revenue suggestions, and day-to-day operational musts in order to have everyone on the same page concerning what needed to be done.

1. Weekly staff meetings were arranged that incorporated agendas, a time limit, new business and old business, and a "what if" dreaming session to brainstorm new products. They satisfied all

concerned and put a stop to the previous "implied" communication style.
2. No new products were accepted or produced until they met the criteria of new product development. When a new product was initiated, it was thoroughly announced, thoroughly defined, and was attached to a revenue projection.
3. A cross-training program for all positions was initiated from CEO to receptionist. All positions could now be covered, no matter what the emergency.
4. Monthly company gatherings were planned to tell people about successes and failures, to get people excited and to motivate them to buy into new projects.

Marie improved her leadership traits 100 percent by being more aware of employee needs, wants, and capabilities. The company continues to turn out a large group of new products each year, but they do it successfully with effective procedures, informed employees, and published revenue projections.

Leadership Traits Improved because of: Enthusiasm, Caring, Trusting, Being Strategic, Doing the Numbers, Discipline, Listening and Communicating

The Hurt Feelings Leader*sm*:

I've owned my own business for 17 years as a management consultant and have been an executive coach for nine of those 17 years. Women are now 70 percent of my consultancy and coaching practice. In my opinion and experience, the number one non-leadership trait that women managers and leaders demonstrated is that of "hurt feelings" or taking their work or decisions personally. The inability to move past their personal feelings and reactions has kept many women from being highly effective, strategic leaders and trusted as decision makers.

As a woman, I want to be very clear about the issue I am discussing here. It is not that women are too emotional, although we have been accused of that since the beginning of time. (I've also experienced highly emotional men in situations that called for high emotion.) The point I want to make about taking things personally and having hurt feelings is that you can rarely be effective and strategic if your feelings are always in your way.

I currently work with several high-level women leaders who are learning to move from believing that situations are their fault to dealing with business issues in need of their leadership. The distinction between thinking of an issue as your fault and managing an issue based on what is needed at the time is a huge leap for many women.

Clarity, workmanship, effectiveness, strategic planning, shipping of product, meeting deadlines, managing employees, and keeping the team effective is a group and/or organizational dynamic. There is never one person responsible for the whole problem.

Allowing yourself to be hurt — personally hurt — for a missed deadline, is to undermine your self-confidence. If you were responsible for something not working well, then investigate what went wrong, find out what your responsibility or contribution to the error is, repair it as best you can, and then move on.

Many women leaders are reluctant to move up the ranks of management into leadership positions because of all the possibilities of doing something wrong, as if being "wrong" is something to avoid completely.

Failure, missed deadlines, mistakes, errors, and wrong decisions are all part of managing and leadership. It is rare that a new product or service is perfectly planned and executed. More often than not, errors provide the means of making the product or service better, faster, newer.

You cannot avoid errors. The feeling of not wanting to make mistakes — to protect yourself personally from making errors — will keep you from thinking clearly and thus leading well. Instead, you will avoid decision making, hesitate to get a job done, worry about what others think, and agonize over decisions once they are made.

"How do I stop taking things personally?"

Understand what your contribution is to the situation. Do the best you can with the information at hand and take action. If you create a reputation for good solid research, communicating concerns, developing a sense of urgency, and then supporting the decision, you will become a true leader in a short period of time.

Leadership is a responsibility and a gift. It is entrusted to you by people who feel you can help make them successful and/or can help make the organization successful. They follow your lead because they desire to be like you, think like you, work like you, and lead like you. They trust your method of working and want to support it.

Here are some very clear and concise questions you can ask yourself before you take anything personally. These questions will help you move past the hurt and into the strategic arena of leadership.

a. What is the problem here?
b. What is my contribution to the problem?
c. What can and should be done immediately to correct the problem?
d. Whom can I ask about this problem?
e. What information am I missing that I need to correct this problem?

There is no personal hurt expressed here. The questions are logical and strategic and will help you to determine what the needs are. You won't have to worry about who likes you, who thinks you are not good at what you do, or who is trying to make you look bad.

The process of asking these questions — taking a step back and breathing deeply — will definitely align you with the ranks of other good leaders. Let me give you a very stark example of leadership and being a team player. This is a true story.

Remember This Woman's Story

For six months an executive team of nine men and one woman worked on the strategic business development plans for a multi-billion dollar corporation. They would meet in the board room each week for hours mulling over documents, reviewing research and records, examining spread sheets and cash flow analysis and developing a plan for their future. The plan they were developing would cover the next 2-4 years of business.

This 10-person team, including the CEO of the corporation, worked diligently for six months to put together a viable, workable and profitable business plan for their corporation's future.

At the end of the six months and with the launch of the new business plan, it was decided by the team that one of the team members would be eliminated. Although it was not a solution that everyone agreed with, it was a team decision and the person was let go.

The final business development meeting ended. All members of the team left the room except for the woman and the CEO. She asked the CEO if she could have a few minutes with him to give him some feedback. This is what she said to him:

"I do not think our decision to let one of our team members go is a good one. I think we should reconsider the decision."

When the woman had her performance review the next month, she was rated as insubordinate and was let go within the next few months from her position and from the company.

Do you know why?

The CEO could no longer trust her, she showed herself to not be a team player and she undermined the entire business plan by not abiding by the team decision.

Personal feelings should not be the deciding factor in business decisions. When you look at all the contributing factors to a decision, including how it will affect the employee population or the organization, and make a decision, your personal feelings need to be removed.

This concept can be the most difficult for new and established women leaders to learn: A decision is a decision. Teamwork is more important than personal feelings. The good of the whole organization is the ultimate goal.

Leadership as a Way of Being:

After 17 years in business, I receive referrals from people who want to become more effective and increase their revenues. As we begin to have a conversation about how to proceed, it becomes evident to me that I am dealing with some very talented people who don't yet recognize their personal professional assests.

Leaders are made. Very few people are born as leaders. Leaders learn by doing, watching, learning, failing and trying again. Failure is a superb leader-maker. And the more you fail, and get up, and try again, the better leader you will be.

Leading is not about perfection. The executives, CEOs, and professionals that I am privileged to work with can sometimes have this idea that the leaders in "the books" or in the other companies are better and smarter than they are. It is usually not true.

Here is my unscientific research (but real life experience) about people who strive to be leaders of their lives, communities and professions.

Leaders Care. They care deeply about the process of the project, the needs of the people, and the desires of the stakeholders and customers.

Leaders Create Trust. Leaders create an atmosphere of trust by keeping their word, revealing what needs to be done, allowing for change, and asking for help when needed. They also ask for input into strategic decisions and take the heat when the going gets tough. People work harder, longer and with greater heart for people they trust.

Leaders Create Opportunity. I admire leaders so much in this arena because it would be so easy to move forward with bright ideas in a timely way and not stop for others to step on board the learning train. Leaders recognize when others need to learn, grow, be trained, be heard and contribute. And in recognizing the need to create opportunity and supporting it, they create loyalty from the people they lead.

Leaders Are Innovators. The word innovation is synonymous with failure, error, mistake, "holy Toledo" and "oh no." Innovation requires real courage and the willingness to take risks. Leaders move in the direction of new products, new services, untried concepts, and untried territories. What results from this courage and risk taking is all around us: the internet, digital technology, microwaves, the Mars space probe, and a million products that are a part of our everyday lives.

Yes, you are a Leader

Patricia and Tim became leaders. Marie became a leader. And my Hurt Feelings manager became a leader. They have the willingness to take a good long look at what they are creating, how it is working (or not), and how to apply their talents with the proven Leadership Traits to help them grow into more productive and polished leaders.

Find an example of a leader you admire and then examine why. I think you will find that at the core of this person is someone who cares deeply about the end result and certainly about the process of getting to that end result.

Competent leaders are made. They are formed of the daily grind, and the willingness to look at their missing leadership traits develop them, and practice them whenever they can.

I have the privilege of working with and coaching so many emerging leaders. I bet if you take a close look, you will see that you, too, are an emerging leader.

This work is dedicated to my girls, Natalie Jr. and Shannon, who taught me everything I needed to know about leadership.

About Natalie Manor

*N*atalie Manor brings clarity and leverage in her *Strategies for Success*^{sm} to her clients and audiences. She provides the means to develop extraordinary, high value relationships — both personally and professionally — in order to become superior performers. She is an executive coach, consultant, speaker and co-author of Wholehearted Success *and* Give Stress a Rest. *She offers powerful, practical and on-target advice for mastering executive and team excellence, executive skill building and communication. Natalie also instructs on corporate workplace issues, with an emphasis on developing executive women.*

Her KICKS audio tapes have been endorsed internationally in publications such as Entrepreneur, Self, Runners World, USA Today, Kiplinger's, Prevention, Men's Health, *and* Paul Harvey's Report. *She has appeared on BBC's* AllNight *and on hundreds of radio and TV stations. Natalie stays current with memberships in the National Speakers Association, International Coaching Federation and American Society for Training and Development.*

Contact Information:
Natalie Manor
Natalie Manor & Associates
P.O. Box 1508
Merrimack, NH 03054
Phone: (603) 424-7700
Fax: (603) 424-1267
E-mail: CoachNatalie@NatalieManor.com
Website: www.NatalieManor.com

THE 1% LEADER

by Michael Connor

Horsies

It was spring and there was a carnival in town. It was one of those small weekend carnivals with a dozen rides and few booths, but it was our two-year old daughter's first real taste of a merry-go-round. The following day, Monday, she wanted to go back and see the horsies. I tried to explain to her that the fair had moved on to another town, but she'd have none of it. Eventually she wore me down with her persistent statements of "Let's check, daddy" and "Maybe the horsies are still there." I decided to drive by where the carnival had been on my way to pick up the babysitter, so she could actually see the vacant lot and be satisfied the horsies were no longer there.

We drove by the lot, now empty, and my daughter asked, once again, "Where did they go?" I tried to explain, once again, that they had moved on to another town, so that other children would also get the chance to go on the rides. On the way to get the babysitter, my daughter continued, with innocent tenacity, her quest to find the horsies, stating "Maybe we can find them, daddy" and "We can go to another town, too." I was in the middle of explaining to her why it was highly unlikely that we'd see any horsies on our way to pick up the babysitter, when I stopped myself. Why, I wondered, do I feel the need to dampen her enthusiasm about seeing more horsies? How do I know where the fair is? Who knows? Maybe we will see some horsies.

The moment after I opened my mind to the possibility of horsies at 8 a.m. on a Monday morning and joined my daughter's enthusiasm, we passed a nearby mall. I glanced over and saw, you guessed it, horsies! I made a quick u-turn and pulled into the mall parking lot, where carnival workers were assembling rides, including a merry-go-round.

As we spent a few minutes enjoying our little Monday morning miracle together, I wondered whether or not I would have seen the horses if I hadn't shifted my attitude from we won't see them to maybe we will. I began considering all the areas of my life where I block out opportunities and possibilities because my experience and beliefs tell me they are unlikely or impossible. I looked back over at my daughter and marveled in the gift she had just given me.

The 1% Miracle

I'm not sure to whom to attribute the following quote. I heard it from a colleague and a friend who, I'm sure, picked it up from another. Nonetheless, it has provided me with a foundation for living life.

When you give 50%, you get 50% in return;
When you give 75%, you get 75% in return;
When you give 90%, you get 90% in return;
When you give 99%, you get 99% in return;
When you give 100%, you get The Whole Universe in return.

What does it mean to give 100%? What does it mean to let go of that last shred of doubt or resistance and step across that chasm from 99% to 100%? Those who have made the 1% leap know it. Those who have not, I invite to explore it. 1% leaders have experienced 100% because they've trusted themselves enough to take that leap. Words can't adequately capture its magnitude. What does it mean to believe so fully, to be committed so completely, to be aligned so clearly that one literally taps into the power, creativity, and assistance of the Universe?

Ponder that question while I share another story with you.

A Matter of Perspective in Bulgaria

Blagoevgrad is a town of 60,000, two hours south of Sofia, the capital of Bulgaria. It sits at the foothills of the breathtaking Purin and Rila mountain ranges. The local soccer team's stadium served as my morning exercise site while I lived there. I found myself running up and down the steps of the stadium on a cool February morning, faced with a decision.

Having recently arrived from the United States as a consultant to the Bulgarian Ministry of Health and having taken the initial steps to evaluate the condition of the local hospital and the needs of its management team, I was becoming increasingly clear on one simple, albeit profound, truth. If external change is not matched with a corresponding inner shift of beliefs, then the changes won't last long.

I had gained the respect of the management team, consisting primarily of the medical director and other influential physicians within the hospital, rather quickly and we had, together, developed a plan to address some of the organization's more apparent needs. Several days later, two of these physicians appeared at my office door looking somewhat despondent. They explained to me that the regulations established by the Ministry of Health wouldn't allow us to implement our plan. Along with their disappointment, I also sensed a sort of relief, as if they had found a viable reason not to pursue our plan, which, for them, was a sharp deviation from the routine they'd been practicing for years. I requested a copy of the regulations so I could better understand what we were up against.

Having spent nearly a decade in health care in the States and having become accustomed to the endless process of staying current with, deciphering, and working with health care regulations and regulators, I fully expected volumes of detailed regulations to arrive on my desk. Not only was I dealing with a former communist county, but with a health care system that had changed little in the interim. Certainly I could expect even stronger, more detailed regulations in this country where controlling human behavior, rather than expanding human potential, was the guiding principle.

To my amazement, I was presented with an 8 by 10 booklet. When I assumed this was some type of summary and asked where the rest of the regulations were, I was even more startled to be informed that these were, in fact, all of the regulations. Upon being asked to point out the specific regulation that was troublesome to our plan, my Bulgarian colleagues seemed confused, as if not understanding my question. They identified several problematic regulations, which, upon translation, didn't appear to be issues to me.

In the ensuing discussion, a light went off in my head. I began to see that we were coming from totally different viewpoints. I assumed we could do anything unless told otherwise, whereas they assumed we could do something only if the regulations gave us the permission. According to their way of thinking, if it's not stated in the regulations, you can't do it.

As this awareness began to sink in, the magnitude of its implications, not just for the management team at the hospital but for the entire society, became clearer. How could I possibly hope to make any substantial progress working with a mindset deeply rooted in the belief that external permission must precede initiative?

Tempted to pack up my bags and go home, I instead shifted my focus to addressing these core belief structures. Almost immediately I thought of a seminar I had taken several years earlier that powerfully and effectively addressed these paradigms and patterns of thinking that were deeply rooted in my Bulgarian colleagues. The more I thought about the seminar, the more it seemed like a perfect fit for this situation. The problem, of course, was actually making such a seminar happen in Bulgaria.

That morning running on the steps in the soccer stadium, the decision before me was whether or not to commit my efforts to plan, promote, and organize an intensive six-day seminar. Doing so meant flying in a trained facilitator and a team of ten assistants, finding an adequate space, promoting and marketing a totally new form of training in a former communist country, and establishing an office to work out of — all within four months and with no budget. I had also been in the country for less than a month and could neither speak nor understand the language. Sound crazy?

A Leap of Faith

The only thing pulling me towards this insane undertaking was that I really, really wanted to do it. I wanted to do it because I felt it was essential and foundational to any long-term progress. I wanted to do it because I felt if we did one training, there might be more to follow and that I might light a spark that could turn into a great fire of awareness and effectiveness. I wanted to do it because I wanted to do what seemed, on the surface, to be impossible. I wanted to do it because I felt it was the greatest service I could provide to the people of Blagoevgrad and Bulgaria. I wanted to do it because, when I was really honest with myself, I knew if I chose less, I would experience and see myself as less.

So, somewhere towards the end of my workout, I got clear that there was really only one choice that was truly on-purpose for me. I walked back to my apartment totally certain that we would be doing a successful, nationally promoted seminar in four months but without the foggiest notion how that was going to happen.

You've likely seen the quote below before, but none better captures the essence of the 1% Miracle and my experience in Bulgaria. If you've seen it before, do your best to read it as if you're reading it for the first time. Be the child who knows that horsies are everywhere, not the adult who dismisses anything "fanciful" or "unreasonable." The miracle of 100% is rarely born of logic.

> *"Until one is committed there is hesitancy,*
> *the chance to draw back, always ineffectiveness.*
>
> *Concerning all acts of initiative (and creation),*
> *there is one elementary truth, the ignorance of which kills*
> *countless ideas and splendid plans:* ***that the moment***
> ***one definitely commits oneself, then Providence moves too.***
>
> *All sorts of things occur to help one that would never otherwise*
> *have occurred. A whole stream of events issues from the decision,*
> *raising in one's favor all manner of unforeseen incidents*
> *and meetings and material assistance, which no man could have*
> *dreamt would have* come his way.
>
> *I have learned a deep respect for one of Goethe's couplets:*
>
> *Whatever you can do, or dream you can, begin it.*
> *Boldness has genius, power and magic in it!"*
>
> — W. B. Murray,
> The Scottish Himalayan Expedition, 1950

None of the unforeseen incidents, meetings, and material assistance referred to by Murray are possible at 99%. I had no Plan B for the seminar. We were doing a seminar, no matter what. Had I had the slightest crack in my commitment, it surely would have been exposed in the next four months.

A Test of Commitment

As if in response to my clear commitment, a number of things fell into place quickly. I was able to secure a facilitator who was willing to come at a reduced fee. I found a location and a translator and made arrangements to use a local university's office to handle administrative details and registrations. Anyone who's undertaken a venture knows, however, that the rubber meets the road when it comes to sales and financing. I needed paying customers in the room to offset my expenses. This meant convincing people whose monthly income averaged $20 to pay two months' worth of wages for a six-day training they'd never heard of before, when all their previous training and education had been supported by the state, at no expense to them. Not an easy sell.

I got myself on national radio, I spoke at conferences, I printed brochures and reached out to everyone I knew. I even went to a foundation and requested a grant, although I had no officially recognized organization or sponsor backing me. After doing everything I knew to do, I found myself two weeks before the seminar with revenue projections at 20% of what I needed to offset my expenses. It wasn't so much that people weren't interested, they just weren't able or willing to pay the full tuition to attend.

The facilitator had already booked his flight from the States. We had assistants coming from three different continents. We had incurred printing, translation, promotion, and travel expenses, and had committed to use and pay for the space. I was in Sofia a week before the seminar trying to figure out how I would handle the expenses. I felt in-over-my-head and there was no turning back. Self-doubt and fear crept in. Insecurity began to taint my thoughts. I feared the whole thing would be a bust, and I would be the fool who had attempted something impossible and, of course, failed.

Then something shifted, as if a powerful force came forward from within, bigger than the doubt, the fear, the money, or even the seminar. I was committed to and acting on the very thing that, in my heart, I believed in! I was living life fully, going for what was most important for me. I was doing something wonderful and exciting. I'd contact friends and family back home for loans to pay the bills if I needed to, but we were doing a seminar — and it was going to be great!

Upon returning to the hospital in Blagoevgrad the following day, my interpreter, who had been a huge support throughout the process, informed me that a postcard had arrived for me and was on my desk. The tone of her voice and the look in her eyes filled me with anticipation. I went to my office, read the postcard, and wept. To my amazement, the foundation that I applied to, with no organizational backing or sponsors, had approved my grant in full. It was exactly what I needed to pay for all the seminar-related expenses.

The seminar went beautifully and was so well received by those participating that they requested more seminars. Now, ten years later, the seminars continue in Bulgaria, run by Bulgarians who have learned to take initiative, believe in themselves, and commit themselves fully to what matters most to them.

The 1% Leader

What do seminars in Bulgaria, Himalayan Expedition leaders, and merry-go-rounds have in common? First and foremost, something that really, really matters. A desire or a wanting that is neither born in the intellect nor motivated primarily by money. My daughter really, really wanted to see horsies again. Murray really, really wanted to climb Mount Everest. I really, really wanted to bring a seminar to Bulgaria.

Secondly, each of the above examples is similar in that the commitment was made without knowing how the result would be created. 1% Leaders don't allow methods to muddy their vision or obstacles to dampen their dreams. They know that everything necessary for success will show up along the way when they are willing to commit themselves fully.

1% Leaders understand one important distinction about commitment: *You can't commit to what you're not committed to already.* 1% Leaders understand that the only way to believe so fully, to be committed so completely, and to be aligned so clearly that one taps into the power, creativity, and assistance of the Universe is by knowing what truly matters most to them. A "commitment" for any other reason is not a true commitment. A goal, intention, or dream maybe, but not a commitment.

A commitment, as defined by 1% Leaders, has no maybe in it. Because it comes forward from the deepest place of purpose within, it tends to generate enthusiasm, anticipation, and adventure, rather than a sense of obligation or unwanted responsibility. 1% Leaders are never motivated by a "should" or "have to," and they understand that every commitment is, in fact, a commitment to themselves. They understand, usually experientially and sometimes intellectually, that a true commitment includes the heart, mind, and body. The heart holds our deepest purpose and truest desires and values. The mind formulates and implements the plan. Our actions, aligned with our purpose and plan, complete the cycle and open the space for the Universe to work with and through us.

More importantly, 1% Leaders also support others in their organizations and on their teams in clarifying what matters most to them and committing only to those projects, activities, and undertakings that line up with their deepest sense of purpose. They understand that any other approach is, ultimately, counterproductive. They understand that people operating at a true 100% will not only enjoy the thrill of the journey, but will also manifest results exponentially greater than those operating at 99% or less.

The primary motivator for assisting others in experiencing 100%, however, is that 1% Leaders really, really want to. They thrill in the process of assisting and supporting others in being the very best they can be. It is, simply, who they are.

The Hologram

Shine an image through a hologram and the result is a three-dimensional image in space. Break the hologram into pieces and shine the same image through any one of the pieces, and, amazingly, you get the same three-dimensional image. It's as if the entire hologram is in each of the pieces. The whole is in all of the parts.

1% Leaders know that each one of us is like a piece of the hologram. The whole is within each of us. When we're willing to trust ourselves and leap that last 1% into total commitment, the illusion of smallness is lifted and the entire Universe, that was there all along, presents itself in all its magnificence and glory.

The Whale

Allow me to conclude with one more brief story about my daughter, that wonderful teacher of mine. Last summer we spent several weeks at our favorite lake in upstate New York. My daughter had a number of new beach toys, including a series of plastic aquatic animals. I noticed, at one point, that the blue whale had been missing for several days. I asked my daughter where it was and got no reply.

The following day as my wife was leaving the beach, my daughter said, "Mommy, wait." She was digging a hole in the sand with her shovel, and, I assumed, simply wanted her mother to stay around a bit longer. My wife started up the steps towards our cabin, and my daughter again asked her to wait. Finally, about six inches under the surface, she struck something with her shovel. Clearly left days before in the surf, the blue whale emerged.

How did she know it was there?

About Michael Connor

*M*ichael Connor is the President of Creative Transitions: Transforming Challenges into Opportunities, a company specializing in assisting organizations, teams, and individuals in thriving, excelling, and profiting in the midst of change. He has designed and presented keynotes and trainings worldwide since 1993, including his acclaimed "1% Miracle" and "1% Leader" programs. Mike is the former President and CEO of the Insight Educational Institute. A former health care executive with a wealth of business and management expertise, Mike has presented on four continents. He holds Masters Degrees in Health Care Management and Practical Theology. While consulting to the Ministry of Health in Bulgaria, he met his wife, Maria, a physician. The parents of two children, they live near Boston.

Contact Information:
Michael Connor
Creative Transitions
8 Nauset Road
Brockton, MA 02301
Phone: (508) 584-9062
Fax: (508) 580-6466
E-mail: MC@ThriveOnChange.com
Website: www.ThriveOnChange.com

Leadership is an Art ...
Not a Position

by Bonnie Dean

"Of all the things I've done, the most vital is coordinating the talents of those who work for us and pointing them toward a certain goal."
— *Walt Disney*

Leadership has been described as the art of inspiring people to undertake an adventure in pursuit of a common goal. Magnetic leadership begins with a vision of the future; it has energy and starts in the right side of the brain. It challenges and encourages people to look beyond the immediate and to envision future possibilities and change. Magnetic leadership inspires others to strive for a bold, common goal, a desired outcome, and sets the tone and the direction as it models the behaviors for ordinary people to achieve extraordinary results. Magnetic leadership involves the head and the heart. It arouses passion in the people it attracts.

According to the Bible, "without dreams and visions we perish." Leaders need a compelling vision of clear goals and a flair for communicating that vision to a broad range of people in a manner they all can understand. Magnetic leaders are consistent. They stand firm in their values so their team always knows what to expect and what is expected.

"The true sign of a good teacher is not how many students she has, rather how many begin to teach. The sign of an effective leader is not how many follow...it is how many begin to lead."
— Bonnie Dean

Let's look at the difference between leadership and management. Management is focused on structure, processes, discipline, control, and results. It originates in the left side of the brain and allows people to assert their vision by means of marshaling and strong-arming to deploy resources. It is about keeping track of numbers, incremental improvements, doing things right, not making mistakes, and the predictable outcomes are no major breakthroughs, complacency, and high levels of mediocrity. We have all witnessed highly managed companies that have self-destructed due to lack of leadership.

A Carnegie Foundation study found that success in life is based 15 per cent on technical skills and 85 percent on our ability to manage ourselves and our ability to communicate well with others. (*Note it didn't say manage others!) People join organizations looking for leadership; they leave because of managers.

During the past two decades of professional speaking, training teams, facilitating retreats, and conducting PowerTeam events, I have discovered a few universal truths that magnetic leaders seem to innately know. People will join, stay, and flourish within any type of team structure (i.e., career/office, board of directors, charity, church, or family) for three basic reasons:

1. The sense of belonging to something bigger than themselves.
2. The sense that they are learning and growing from their affiliation.
3. The sense that they are contributing and that their contribution is appreciated.

When any of these three reasons falls away, so does the team member from his career, job, and other personal and professional affiliations. Leaders of staff offices, sales teams, committees, classrooms, and households are eager for ways to communicate more effectively with their team members and to focus on creating prosperity through people in all arenas of their lives. We live in a high-tech/low-touch world; however, as the amount of information and technology that enters the workplace doubles and triples, the need for the human element — magnetic leadership — increases as dramatically.

Communicating may be defined as connecting. The foundation of leadership is built on the quality of our ability to communicate/connect with others. Two elements in life that have a major impact on the art of leadership are the people we meet and the books we read. I have provided a list at the end of this chapter of books that have helped me shape my leadership style and communication skills. Enjoy! With those resources in place to take each of these points to a deeper level, here is a simple, three-step system that embraces the elements of a magnetic leader.

1. Focus on Relationship Power

According to Tom Peters, we all have over one thousand opportunities every day to affect others through our communication with them. We affect them whether we are aware of it or not. Just as we know that people want to do business with people they like and trust, people flourish when working in an environment with people that like and trust them as well.

There are words in our language that set up roadblocks and shut down channels of communication between individuals. Likewise, there are words that open us up at a heart and soul level and encourage connecting. These words may seem elementary, but as Stephen Covey says, "Just because something is common sense doesn't mean it's common practice."

The 21 Most Important Words to Use When Leading Others
The Six Most Important Words

I admit I made a mistake. This phrase makes you human and sets the stage for others to admit they make mistakes too. Lots of room for teams to grow in this environment. Mistakes help us learn what doesn't work and become more creative in looking for solutions in the future.

"In times of rapid change, experience can be your worst enemy."
— J. Paul Getty

The Five Most Important Words

You did a great job! No one suffers from too much recognition or praise. It is amazing to me that the only time you hear some managers say "well done" is when they order a steak in a restaurant. The best way to acknowledge people is in front of their peers. A little bit of praise goes a long way in making others want to be a part of your team. Don Peterson, the former CEO of Ford Motor Company, says, "The most important ten minutes of your day are the ones you spend boosting the morale of the people around you!"

> *"If you are in harmony with yourself, you may meet a lion without fear. He respects anyone with self-confidence."*
>
> — Nelson Mandela

The Four Most Important Words

What is your opinion? People will tell us the most incredible things when we take the time to ask with genuine interest and then make time to listen with our ears, hearts, and eyes to their answers. (*Check out the book F.I.S.H. for ways to "Be There" for others.)

> *"I am convinced that if the rate of change inside an organization is less than the rate of change outside, the end is in sight."*
>
> — Jack Welch

The Three Most Important Words

Let's do it! Not, you do it, or get out of my way — no one can do it as well as I — when the emphasis in not on who takes credit, teams move forward at a faster pace.

> *"I am just a plow hand from Arkansas, but I learned how to hold a team together, how to lift some men up, how to calm others, until finally they've got one heartbeat together as a team. There's just three things I'd ever say: If anything goes bad, I DID IT. If anything goes semi-good, then WE DID IT. If anything goes real good, YOU DID IT! That's all it takes to get people to win football games for you."*
>
> — Bear Bryant

The Two Most Important Words

Thank you! Practice this one at home, on the most important people in your life, and see the response you get.

> *"Attitude reflects leadership"*
>
> — From the movie *Remember the Titans*

The Most Important Word

We There is no mistake our Pledge of Allegiance begins with "I" and ends with "liberty and justice for all." This is the mentality of magnetic leaders.

"Leadership is the art of getting someone else to do something you want done because he wants to do it."

— Dwight D. Eisenhower

Imagine that all of us on this planet walk around with huge invisible buttons on our chests that say, "Make me feel important." A good question to ask yourself is, "What can I do to make my associates feel important today?" There is an A.L.E.R.T. factor that magnetic leaders embody. We all have a deep need to be acknowledged, listened to, encouraged, respected, and treated to genuine praise. These are deposits you can put into the emotional bank accounts of others that pay huge dividends in the way others respond to you as a leader, parent, partner, associate, and friend. Incorporate these words and actions into your daily routines at home and at work, and watch your teams rise to the standards and expectations that you set.

Acknowledgement

Listen

Encourage & Support

Respect

Treat to genuine praise

2. Utilize the Art of Delegation

Magnetic leaders concentrate on bringing out the best in the people around them. They do this by giving ownership of the ultimate goal to the team.

"If you want to build a ship, don't drum to the women and men to gather wood, and give orders. Instead, teach them to yearn for the vast and endless sea."

— Antoine De Saint-Exupery

Share the knowledge of how to do it rather than trying to do it all yourself, even if you think you can do it better or faster. Find others on your team who will grow personally and professionally on the road to becoming future leaders in your organization. The first question you need to ask yourself is: "Who else could do this job?" The second, more important, question is: "Who on my team could benefit from learning how to do this, and who would enjoy doing it?" Utilize team members so they are constantly learning and growing from their association with you.

"Every person I work with knows something better than me. My job is to listen long enough to find it and use it."

— Jack Nicklaus

Every leader is responsible for creating an environment where people can blend business values with values held by individuals. Rob LeBow was the marketing leader with Bill Gates in the 70s and 80s. His "Eight Principles of the Heroic Environment" demonstrate how Microsoft blended shared values.

The Eight Principles of the Heroic Environment

1. Treat others with uncompromising truth.
2. Lavish trust on your associates.
3. Mentor unselfishly.
4. Be receptive to new ideas, regardless of their origin.
5. Take personal risks for the organization's sake.
6. Give credit where credit is due.
7. Do not touch dishonest dollars.
8. Put the interests of others before your own.

What will it take to create a Heroic Environment in your organization?

An exercise designed to help you better understand the values and beliefs people bring to the team is to have each member spend approximately 3-5 minutes answering the following questions, and then sharing the answers as a group. Encourage participants to give an immediate response and not to share answers until you come back together as a group. People connect quickly, at a deeper level of trust and understanding, when they share values that are important to them in an environment where their opinions are given respect and listened to.

1. A person will work hard if _____.
2. People will cooperate with one another when_____.

3. Personal success can be measured by _____.
4. I usually get the best results by _____.
5. When I think something needs to be said I _____.
6. My greatest frustration is _____.
7. Others would describe me as _____.
8. The thing about myself I value most is _____.
9. The quality I value most in others is _____.
10. If I could change one thing here it would be _____.
11. I am happiest when _____.
12. I am most responsible when _____.

In the art of delegation, the first question you need to ask yourself is: "Who else could do this job?" The second, more important, question is: "Who on my team could benefit from learning how to do this, and who would enjoy doing it?" Utilize team members so they are constantly learning and growing from their association with you. Study the personality styles of your people to understand their strengths and weaknesses and delegate responsibilities to build on team strengths. (Check out book list — *The Platinum Rule* — for a valuable resource in this arena.) Leaders use delegation to develop future leaders and to free themselves for the art of leadership, which includes reflective thinking, planning, and the five F's.

The Five F's of Magnetic Leadership

Future Focused — Ability to project into the future, constantly pushing the vision ahead as they near their goals. A magnetic leader gets the team even more excited about the vision than he or she is!

"*Unusual wisdom is foreseeing what is going to happen. Study market trends, take inventory, reexamine your values, and create a new vision that positions YOU as a leader.*"

— Marilyn Manning

Fast Acting — Able to make quick decisions, to be creative and to take risks . . . encouraging their team to do the same with the goal of constant and never- ending improvement. A part of the art of this F is honoring mistakes as ways not to do something. Recognize the error and move on together! Remember, magnetic leaders work to create success for others because that results in success for the organization.

Focused on Influence rather than Control — Understanding that the only control we have is how we respond to the stress in our day-to-day lives, and that we influence the people around us by the manner in which we respond. Are we mentors or tormentors? Are we exhibiting traits that we are proud of and qualities we want our teams to emulate?

"You need clarity on your own non-negotiables. You need to know what you won't budge on, or you'll be buffeted by the winds."
— Curtis Berrien

Filters — People share with leaders the most unbelievable information. Do we place ourselves above the gossip and put the interests of our team first? Leaders are able to sit on information or situations for 24-48 hours. Most problems brought to the attention of a leader work themselves out in that time frame. A magnetic leader earns respect by listening, filtering what was said and not over-reacting to people's emotions and situations.

Balance — We are not so much victims of our circumstances as we are of our priorities.

Friendly Tutors — Constantly challenging those around them to stretch and grow. The leaders who stand out in my mind are those who challenged their people to promote right past them and meant it! It is about putting the well-being of your team ahead of your self-interests. When I lived in Southern California, we had a young father of four next door. He never mowed the lawn, fixed a drain, or mended a fence without teaching one of the kids how to do it, and then he got out of their way while they worked. I marveled at his patience, expertise, and art of leadership!

The smartest way to delegate to others is by giving them as much information, up front, as possible. The more your people understand, the less supervision or persuasion they will need. In the 2002 movie *K-19: The Widowmaker*, Liam Neeson plays Captain Polenin, a commander of a Russian nuclear submarine. His loyalty to his men over country is questioned, so the ship's command is turned over to Captain Vostrikow, played by Harrison Ford. Vostrikow is a slave driver — never connecting with his crew, demanding and alienating in his brash, by-the-book manner. When it appears all is lost and he starts to tell the crew that they all must die, the demoted Captain Polenin pleads with him; "Don't tell them ... ASK them. They are your men ... they will make the right decision, they will follow you."

It takes courage to make changes. "Recognize that every 'out front' maneuver you make is going to be lonely. If you feel entirely comfortable you're not far enough ahead to do any good. That warm sense of everything going well is usually the temperature at the center of the herd."
— Anonymous

The art of leadership has to do with being a "human highlighter" by bringing the best out in those you work, play, live with, by sharing responsibility, risk, and reward, and by giving them ownership of the results so that they feel good about their role in the adventure and grow due to their exposure to your leadership.

3. Never Dwell on Past Problems

Take a lighter attitude of the whole process. We cannot move forward when we are stuck in the past. Set the example as the leader with a positive outlook. Most of us know when we haven't done something well. Catch your team doing things right and let them know you caught 'em! The number one rule of magnetic leadership is: behavior that is rewarded will be repeated. Be careful what you reward. One of my favorite new books on the art of rewarding behavior is *WHALE Done*, by Ken Blanchard. If there is only one other person in your life with whom you would like to develop a more positive relationship, or to merely be more effective at work and at home ... get your hands on this book!

A good question to ask yourself in this area is: "How can we get better?" not, "Who is to blame?" or other negative thoughts. How can we move forward as a team? Who would be a champion in this arena?

Lead your team to constructively solve challenges and acknowledge those who play a role in the end result. At the end of this chapter is a 3-minute problem-solver form. During the years I trained sales teams and middle management, this form was helpful in requiring people to think situations through and creatively come up with solutions before they brought the issue to me.

It gave them an opportunity to take responsibility, be innovative, and think things through before over-reacting. It put an end to chronic complainers and created many humorous outcomes and innovative ideas.

"If you aren't having fun in your work, fix the problem before it becomes serious; Ask for help if you need it. If you can't fix it and won't ask for help, please go away before you spoil it for the rest of us."

— Russ Walden

The first letters of the three steps, *focus, utilize,* and *never* spell **F-U-N!** Your team will strive to emulate a leader who exemplifies an element of fun in the life of their business and in the business of their lives. Don't forget to include your "seventh sense" in your daily routine . . . your sense of humor. Mark Twain said, *"A day is wasted in which I don't laugh."* C.W. Metcalf's book, *Lighten UP,* can help put things into perspective. 9/11 has certainly taught us that our lives can change in an instant. We saw the best in ourselves and our leaders and we witnessed ordinary people rising to the art of extraordinary leadership.

The best way to compete and win in this ever-changing marketplace — and world — is to lead in a value-driven, integrity-based, and nonmanipulative manner to embrace, teach, and acknowledge your team members on their way to understanding the art of leadership in all areas of their lives.

Qualities of a definitive, standout leader of authenticity

1. Communicates well — especially vision/values for the organization
2. Keeps promises
3. Listens
4. Supports the company & staff in word and deed

5. Understands the difference between control and influence
6. Gives credit to the team
7. Makes fair decisions
8. Shares credit, information, and goals
9. Treats others with fairness and respect
10. Keeps a good sense of humor

Magnetic Leadership 3-Minute Problem-Solver Form

To be filled out through "your solution" before being brought to my attention.

Date _____ Time _____ Name _____

Facts _____
_____

Identify Problem _____
_____

*Your Solution _____
_____

Input Received _____
_____

From _____

RESULTS _____
_____

Resources

Allessandra & O'Connor. ***The Platinum Rule.*** Time Warner, 1996.
Best study and explanation of personality styles I have found.

Arrien, Angeles. ***The Four-Fold Way.*** Harper Collins, 1993.
Walking the paths of Warrior, Teacher, Healer and Visionary.

Blanchard, Ken. ***Whale Done!*** The Free Press, 2002.
My favorite new book on fostering positive relationships everywhere.

Bryan, Mark. ***The Artist's Way at Work.*** Quill, 1998.
12 weeks of lessons to creative freedom.

Canfield, Hansen. ***Chicken Soup for the Soul Series.*** Health Communications, Inc. 1993-2002. *Examples of the greatest characteristics leaders can exemplify.*

Dean, Bonnie. ***Give Stress a Rest.*** J&B Publishers, 2001.
Hundreds of ideas on ways to let go and ENJOY more!

DePree, Max. ***Leadership Jazz.*** Dell Publishing, 1992.
ANYTHING by him will propel your leadership style forward!

Dreamer, Oriah Mt. ***The Invitation.*** Harper Collins, 1999.
Take this invitation and your life will never be quite the same.

Giardina, Ric. ***Your Authentic Self.*** Beyond Words Publishing, 2002.
A handbook for being yourself at work and the fulfillment it brings.

Hubbard, Elbert. ***A Message to Garcia.*** Executive Books, (800) 233-2665.
Written in 1899 and as applicable today as ever.

Johnson, Spencer. ***Who Moved My Cheese?*** B.P. Putnam's Sons, 1998.
An A-mazing way to deal with change in work and in life.

LeBow, Rob. **Journey into the Heroic Environment.** Prima Publishers, 1997.
Inside Microsoft leadership.

Lundin, Stephen. ***FISH! (Catch the Energy).*** Hyperion, 2000.
How to release the potential of your team.

Maxwell, John. ***21 Indispensable Qualities of a Leader.*** Thomas Nelson Publishers, 1995. *Becoming the person others will want to emulate!*

Maxwell, John. ***Developing the Leaders Around You.*** Thomas Nelson Publishers, 1999. *How to help others reach their potential.*

Metcalf, C.W. ***Lighten Up. Survival Skills for People Under Pressure.*** Addison-Wesley, 1992. *We can all use this.*

Percy, Ian. ***Going Deep, Exploring Spirituality in Life & Leadership.*** MacMillan, 1997. *A personal favorite — NOT TO BE MISSED!*

St. James, Elain. ***Inner Simplicity*** (series). Hyperion, 1995-2002.

Welch, Jack. ***JACK — Straight From the Gut.*** Warner Business Books, 2001. *Pure Jack! Solid information from a magnetic leader.*

About Bonnie Dean

*B*onnie Dean is the president of W.O.W. Presentations, an international events company that celebrates the relationships of co-workers, customers, and management. Her extensive knowledge of value-based communication skills, team building through creativity and fun, combined with an interactive teaching style and understated sense of humor, create a stimulating learning environment for industry professionals and layman alike. Bonnie has been described as a veg-o-matic blend of Shakespearean actor, improve comic, sitcom starlet, soap opera diva, Vegas showgirl, Harvard professor, informercial huckster, information architect, Broadway choreographer, Navaho storyteller, circus clown, aerobics instructor, and industrial psychologist. She is a human hurricane of immense heart and boundless energy who throws off more sparks than a space shuttle launch. Amazingly, she delivers this entirely on her own with zero help. No computer. No PowerPoint. No special effects. No backup band. Totally unplugged. Her programs include "Together We CAN!," "Why Not You? Why Not Now!," "FowlPlay!," and "GenderBabble." She is the author of Give Stress a Rest and Take It to the Edge!

Contact Information:
Bonnie Dean
W.O.W. Presentations
4840 Fremont Street
Bellingham, WA 98220
Phone: (800) 915-4668
E-mail: Bonnie@BonnieDean.com
Website: www.bonniedean.com

The End of Dominance: The Call for the Multi-Dimensional Leader

by Michelle Cubas

Gain respect effortlessly
Receive recognition humbly
Give empathy without sympathy.
— *Anonymous*

How many times have we asked ourselves quietly and aloud, these questions:

How do I get people to do what I want?
How can I instill a platinum work ethic?
How can I stimulate a leadership legacy?
How can I build equity, beyond the bottom line, into my business?
What part of their day do I offer to my people to find out how they are thinking and feeling about the world?

You're half way to R.O.I. with those questions. Use the next few ideas to add to your R.O.I. — *Your Reality Oriented Investment.*™

Your timing is exceptional for making a difference in business. There is a wave of change, of consciousness, that is founded on how we conduct ourselves as kinder people and more service-oriented professionals. The time is right for the Multi-Dimensional leader.

The Multi-Dimensional Leader is a prism of talents and traits, part:

- Contrarian
- Risk Taker
- Stabilizer
- Innovator

- Visionary
- Model
- Reward Giver
- Director

It's not enough to identify these characteristics. How a person uses them is the real power tool!

Magnetic Leadership is an essential part of Positive Potentials' 10-Point Multi-Dimensional Leadership System™

As a coach to many business leaders, I've identified a leadership model that transcends size, location and adversity.

Multi-Dimensional Leadership Model:

1. Dares to live integrity daily. Has innate balance and resilience (Based on values, consistency is a natural result).
2. Has a strategy to minimize negative influences that result from constant interaction.
3. Possesses uncanny vision and the courage to be different (contrarian).
   - Assesses real issues quickly.
   - Responds appropriately.
   - Uses information to meet the challenges of change.
   - Acquires credentials through enrichment, colleagues and associates.
4. Promotes flexibility and adaptability.
5. Thrives in constant flux.
6. Radiates emotional intelligence and shines it on others.
   - Shares a book, a quote, a movie.
   - Teaches others this acquired skill by simple role modeling this behavior. Gets involved at the seed or root level, such as answering a telephone at the reception desk to hear the reality of what goes on daily.
   - Answers a customer service call and speaks to a real issue. The Multi-Dimensional Leader processes the feeling about the feedback from the customer.

- Has his/her own coach.
- Learns how to share power.
- Develops trust through shared vision. This approach forms the lightning rod during rough challenges.
- Cultivates entrepreneurial energy within the most rigid organization.
- Possesses presence and security to inspire confidence in others.

7. Fosters Business Literacy.™
    - Respects and sponsors lifelong learning and models it.
    - Continually sharpens interpersonal skills.
    - Challenges self with puzzles and problem-solving strategies as part of being and life's strategy.
    - Takes risks and manages errors into the growth process. My coach, Sandra Schrift, quotes Lee Iacocca: "Everything worthwhile carries the risk of failure."
    - Embraces the value of mentoring and professional coaching.
    - Promotes "Acquaintance-Building Programs" that promote understanding and connection — like a foreign exchange program to gain the insight of multiple perspectives.
    - Reinforces cultural sensitivity through personal contact, exposure, and strategic alliances.
    - This posture indicates to all that the company is a global entity and intends to lead rather than follow.
8. Makes decisions founded on long-range value premise and reasonable risk rather than reaction, illusion, and aggrandizement.
9. Productivity for everyone within the leader's sphere of influence.
10. Provides a way for others to follow and be uplifted. They will walk through fire for you. Loyalty is never an issue.

Where Is Leadership When We Need It?

It is concealed within ourselves awakening as the silent revolt begins. Daily media headlines announce shaken foundations of business as we knew it. The business community knows what happens when ethics are absent from an enterprise, be it political, social, or humanitarian.

Americans and global citizens have begun to turn away from the dark road of greed and abuse as a path to power. The demand for effective leadership is no longer an option — it's an absolute. Ethics must return for sensible stability and order to exist.

We're experiencing a mammoth "house cleaning" with the tumble of major corporations. No surprise, however. The foundation was built on a house of cards at the start, nothing substantial and nothing more than greed and power struggles as evidenced by the 1980's mergers and acquisitions mania.

It's almost as though we've stumbled into a darkened corridor and are feeling our way along the wall. A sliver of light is present but we don't know where it's coming from. The corridor could be our human history. The light could be an awakening that intuitively whispers that there is another way.

The state of business today is disgraceful, the epitome of the decay in ethics flowing through the end of the 20th century, which formed a plaque on contemporary life that had to crumble. No surprise.

As industry created disposable products, we transferred disposability to workers. Due to a lack of leadership (no shortage of titles, however), many U.S. companies took unreasonable risks and betrayed the public trust without flinching. The consciences were asleep, lulled by drugs, turmoil, and arrogance on the part of the people at the top.

Simply stated, our biology hasn't caught up with our technology. Science has become the language by which we will manifest our future. But without ethics, our future will be insecure.

There is hope as we strive toward balance. Simultaneously with the tumult, there is an awakening in other areas that can restore faith in our methods and actions. As a species, humans are experiencing a millennium shift in thinking that raises our consciousness. We recognize our unique capacity to apply ourselves, forgive mistakes, and begin anew while releasing the past.

"Of all the creatures of earth, only human beings can change their

patterns. Man alone is the architect of his destiny... Human beings, by changing the inner attitudes of their minds, can change the outer aspects of their lives."

— William James

Leadership Is a Bright Spot in a Dark Place

The Multi-Dimensional Leader has the courage to ask grilling questions and allows an evolution of people and ideas within an open organization. This leader can identify core values and can express them in the business environment. Everyone who connects with the Multi-Dimensional Leader will understand what values to uphold and what the company stands for.

These values are often expressed in mission statements that collect dust on company walls. The life force and energy must be breathed into these statements to achieve purpose and meaning. They have to be *lived* by each company affiliate to be authentic. Life is simpler in companies who do live their values because the values serve as a benchmark of behavior and action which reduces mistakes and upheavals. The participants *know* what is expected, and it is constant.

The Multi-Dimensional Leader identifies needs and values for the universes they govern. This leader identifies and listens to what others must have to be happy, both internally and externally. They are not afraid to encourage inner personal requirements that may include serenity, freedom, love, appreciation, recognition, a voice, honesty, beauty, involvement, creativity, community, and guidance.

Appreciation for these principles flows through a person's lifetime with little modification. They are the filters through which the Multi-Dimensional Leader projects into the future.

Leadership is a mentality
rather than actuality. It is the result of the ultimate self-renewable, role model that avoids burnout because it flows naturally and with ease.

Observable attributes include:
Calm demeanor
Self-referred

Directed by an inner compass
Focused
Resourceful
Compassionate
Passionate
Contemplative
Concerned
Fun

Multi-Dimensional Leadership is a magnet
that attracts and deflects:
  It is self-fulfilling.
  It attracts what is constructive.
  It deflects what is destructive.
  It attracts self-reliant and self-motivated collaborations, people, and resources.
  It is open for input and feedback.
  It is reality-oriented with room to envision the possibilities.

Multi-Dimensional Leadership Blends Passion and Compassion into Values-Driven Leadership

Emergence as a Multi-Dimensional Leader is founded on mastery, not perfection. It is a personal evolution, a result, a continuance that crescendos and sweeps all in the updraft of accomplishment.

The Multi-Dimensional Leader Calls People to

- Daily practice of ethics and code of conduct
- Attention to details: people, process and purpose
- A global perspective from your world to the greater world: how far does the vision reach? Knowing when to think wide and when to think deep
- Courage to be real, flawed, and contrarian
- A balance between risk and reward: an innate sense of timing based on "gut," inner knowing, and sharpened perception
- Possess the "antidote for fear"
- Possess a "nose" for talent: crisp expectations, clear communication, and investment in the future

- Value emotional intelligence over "winning," to be self-paced and resilient
- A new metric for success

The 10/80/10 Principle — The Undertow of Leadership
Knowing when to pick up your basketball and leave!

A coaching colleague, John Brantley, introduced me to a significant idea that finally explains how to attract people who are workable within the organization and why some people won't do what you want. It is called The 10/80/10 Principle.

Volumes have been written on the traits of success. If so much is known, why don't we have greater "success" in our companies? Why are we continuously discussing productivity and excellence if so much is known about them? Can they be that elusive if studied so much?

The visionary leaders already understand the Laws of Attraction, and they want to attract others to their vision. They know that time to market is most important, and they require individuals already prepped for success, not just thinking about it. They don't want to invest in the possibility that someone *might* get it!

Rather than using the Dr. Doolittle *push-me-pull-you* approach, which wastes resources, the enlightened Multi-Dimensional Leader acts as a magnet to attract the qualities, talents, and connections needed in his or her company.

The Multi-Dimensional Leader understands this principle and has no desire to drag people along, but is willing to reach out a hand to pull people up. The Multi-Dimensional Leader recognizes talent and provides a process to groom such individuals. The R.O.I. on such people is enormous.

Invest in the actualizers. It is the keystone for long-term company results. Here are several benefits:
- It generates increased revenue streams for maximum profitability and resilience in volatile markets.
- It uses Business Literacy™ and LaserLearning™ Principles to shorten the company's learning curve (reduce bureaucracy, offer

merit rewards, open input architecture, values innovation).
- Self-referred associates bring freshness to their positions.
- Effortless flow rather than PUSH/PULL is stimulating and self-fulfilling.
- Streamlined and integrated business operations and processes attract people wanting to participate in smoothly run companies. Companies like this are easier for customers and vendors to do business with.
- It inspires all associated with the company to meaningful work and output, referrals, increased sales and branding because everyone talks about how you do business.
- Stimulates flow performance and provides an optimal experience for all associated with you*.

Footnote: *based on Mihaly Csiksentmihalyi work, FLOW, and optimal experience.

The 10/80/10 principle and Business Literacy™ premise are powerful allies. The principle identifies who is in your company. Business Literacy™ discovers and inspires the brain trust to stimulate and ferment growth in the actualizers and 80 percenters.

How these work

The first 10 percent of any group, company, organization, or population, are actualizers. They are self-referred (no prodding is required from outside themselves) and self-starters. The actualizers just need to be pointed in a desired direction with mild reporting points along the path.

They possess the entire spectrum of desired traits our multi-dimensional leader seeks: ethical, resourceful, organized, talented, compassionate and self-motivated. They move forward without being told. They are point-and-shoot ready. Provide the tools, and move aside. They don't need supervision, yet they seek input if they need it. They return with the Gift of Results. They seek solutions, solve their own problems, and self-regulate their time and projects without outside influence.

The last 10 percent in the formula are unsuccessful, regardless of what anyone does. A work horse will never become a thoroughbred, even though it wants to and works hard. All Fords are cars but all cars aren't Fords.

This number can range from 1-10 percent and represents a population of people who will never achieve success. They lack a combination of skills, talents, insight, and beliefs that would advance them. The Multi-Dimensional Leader doesn't try to "fix" these people; the leader offers information and coaching to the highest level that they can use and sends them to a more appropriate environment where they can work.

The core part of the formula is the 80 percent. These people represent a significant ratio of company personnel. They are trainable! They have the raw material and can be molded to the company culture. They will adapt and acquire what the company offers them like a clean slate that has to be written upon. They require attention and training, reinforcement, follow-up, support, and review from the start. They need to know exactly what is required of them so they can perform. They may sprout a few traits of self-starters; however, they need to be coached to a new level.

The "80s" segment benefits from a coaching culture and a multi-dimensional leader's commitment to lifelong learning. The "80s" are most capable of achieving high levels of success within an environment that clearly directs and trains its personnel at all levels. They need the map and a guide.

On the leadership side, when you are consensus building, understanding that 10 percent of the group will support your view, 10 percent will oppose you and 80 percent are waiting to be told which way to go. The 80 percent needs the influence of your leadership.

10/80/10 rule — 10 percent of the population will support you, 10 percent of the population will oppose you, 80 percent are not sure - their minds aren't made up yet.

Don't focus on the 10 percent groups; focus on the 80 percent you can influence.

Example from 52nd Annual Conference Of The International Association of Official Human Rights Agencies (IAOHRA) Renewing Vigilance — Human Rights In The World Community

---

To reduce frustration,
- Acknowledge all the tiers in your organization. Know them for who they are without hoping they will become what they aren't.
- Introduce coaching to the 80 percenters, and let them fly with the support and attention. Enjoy watching some actualizers emerge.
- Reward, tend, and value the actualizers who give pleasure to someone in a leadership position. They make leaders look good within their spheres of influence and keep the pace fluid.

The Roles of the Multi-Dimensional Leader

The Multi-Dimensional Leader creates a work environment that supports all three segments. Not everyone is an actualizer; however, everyone can benefit from a nurturing environment that promotes and stimulates creativity and achievement.

Think of the company as a model family that holds education in high esteem. Grades are never discussed because academic achievement is a value nurtured by the family. The expectations are clear. The rewards and encouragement are plentiful, and there is a climate of fairness, and the ability to learn from mistakes is valued.

A major role of the Multi-Dimensional Leader is to provide certainty in uncertain times. This is accomplished through unbending values and constant reference to the mission statement.

Events are a positive catalyst for the building of employees' personal networks.

Consider coalitions rather than independent stances on common issues. Enrich everyone's experiences through alliances with other departments and businesses.
- Joint events.
- Demonstrate strength in diversity.
- Pool resources — all members benefit.

Working Together — Diversity or Division

Be sensitive to not working in a vacuum to promote isolation. The power of multi-cultural insight and management is money in the bank and an investment and security for your future. Develop sensitivity to multicultural experiences — ready or not, like it or not, here it comes in the 21st century!

Research and invite companies that have done well with multicultural programs. Have them present at an event like a sales meeting where you have a broad audience.
- Who are their audiences?
- Where did they begin?
- What are resources that may apply to your industry and company?
- Teach them how to network.

Plant Values and Virtues in every employee, from the top down.
First step — Definition
- What do you stand for? (quality, service, selflessness, set the example)
- How is your leadership style defined by you?
- How do you provide community support, commitment through the company? (i.e. Employees paid time to volunteer in an organization.)
- What is the organization's personality?
- What can the group accomplish together rather than as individuals?

Second step— Find people who share your values and virtues.
- Recruit to your strongest LINK.
- The prospects have to want and desire to be part of your dream.
- They must want to align their lives with what the company represents.

Third step — Create vision based on values and virtues.
These two qualities prevent erosion of resources and productivity time more than any one element!
- Create and attract profile member from the first outreach through the hiring process as outlined in the next section on vision.

- What do members expect when they join?
- Survey levels of involvement up front. What interests the candidate?
  — Service
  — Recognition
  — Participation earns greater benefits

Fourth step — Set the company's vision.
- Provide clarity, focus, direction, strategy, creativity, faith in the company's future.
- What is the leader's commitment to leaving a legacy?
  — Build it in on the front end.
  — Self-generate growth and retention of personnel through:
    — Recruiting the talent you want.
      — Developing future contacts and vendors through your candidates.
      — Nurturing connections into other companies.
- Offer strong Business Literacy™ requirements

  — Interview for communication skills — listening, verbal, written, presentation. This is where it all starts! You want them already literate in business communications. Use objective experts to locate the talent pool. Otherwise, you'll get "types" the same as the interviewers.

  — Use the Casting Call™ method of interviewing in which candidates audition for their positions

  — Conduct a career audit with the candidate as it relates to your industry, company expectations, crises. What do they already know, read, survey, review?

  — Survey your candidate base to see what they think they need to know.

  — As the final step in the initial interview, state the vision and company goals. Then ask the candidates to align themselves with them.
- Provide a stirring orientation process for new members.
- Print a manual of step-by-step procedures for each department as

baseline expectations and behavior. Leave enough room for the employees to "signaturize" the position they hold so they own it.
- Where do we fit with other companies in our area, other companies who service us? Beyond ranking of sales, consider how many employees have children, how many regularly volunteer, how many are community activists. Make a human connection.
- Inform your employees about the company's corporate giving programs for equipment/sponsorship of special events/organization scholarships. They want to bond with a generous company and will give their loyalty.
- Encourage employees to bring ideas to your attention.
- Bestow a significant annual gift to demonstrate a commitment to a business school of your choice.
- Stimulate employee involvement with giving back to a local school.
- Define team member benefits and flexibility. What makes your company different in care and concern for your personnel?

Attract resources and sponsors that promote your vision.
- Identify community conscious companies that align with your **vision**. Then build an alliance.
- Begin a speakers' bureau from your talent-rich employees.
- Note companies that support your fundraisers.
- Survey marketing groups for the "beat on the street" regarding industry perceptions and your company specifically.
- Encourage and support mentor/intern connections/Shadow Programs.
- Participate in "Nothing Succeeds like Success" programs.
- Members "blaze" a trail of credibility when they excel and others acknowledge it. (community public relations, public appreciation)
- "Barrier Breakers" Awards-acknowledge overcoming adversity
  — Excellence

- Persistence
- Commitment
- Contribution to company
* New employees can compile a quarterly team project of real-world case studies where participants can apply their expertise — marketing, business planning, finance, international business development — and make an instant contribution while learning and participating across department lines.
* Keep research on file for future members.
* Calendar local events available outside of the company.
* Tap into local resources for recruiting, awards and marketing efforts. These are an inexpensive exposure tool to billboard your business message, recruit like-minded people and receive recognition and attention for your company.
  - Public Library
  - Small Business Associations
  - Chambers of Commerce
  - Industry and trade associations

Create a New Metric of Success and Reward

Benefits are only powerful when they are perceived by employees. Find out what's important to them. Maybe they can save or choose an alternative if healthcare is covered by a spouse, for example.

* Negotiate time and resources as perks.
* Define member benefits-insurance, health care, credit union, loan relationships.
* Develop a Process for Establishing Mentor/Intern Connections.
  — Build connections to the "real" world for college graduates.
  — Encourage part-time positions/consistent contacts/service to people as a support person. They are able to try different options.
  — They are already trained in the company culture and they've made an investment of time to work with you.
* How does the company demonstrate a commitment to business studies?

- What does the company give back to the community?
- Reduce attrition and turnover for consistency.

Build Vigor into Your Business Plan
- Nurture successful mind-sets with qualities like optimism, nutrition, fitness, enthusiasm, energy, exuberance, personal development, confidence.
- Create Balance — Keep the balls in the air while avoiding burnout.
- Time management-make events short, worthwhile and interesting.
  — Dynamic event planning
  — Round-table events with business owners — find out what owners are seeking
  — Team building activities

Build Involvement into the Organization
Dynamic event planning is a fun, team-building exercise.
- It can move across departmental lines.
- Make it more than a holiday party!
- Offer community open houses so the neighbors can understand your business — and talk about it!

Volume — Quantity or Quality
Learn the power of exposures — Everyone wants to play on a winning team.

1. Use the media.
2. Present awards/recognition at your company.
3. Invite the community in for events and celebrations.
4. Send clips to share with stakeholders.
5. Have members present in strategic places where there is a large audience.
6. Attend city, county, state government meetings.
7. Attend entertainment venues like community theater.
8. Community visibility projects are essential.

9. Be conscious of strategically placed community investments.
10. Time, energy, money can be well invested in community projects that may have nothing to do with your industry.
11. Name recognition aligned with the community's value. For example, family ties are strong among Hispanics as a community. Be sure to learn something from such a value that you can bring back to your company.

"Interdependent satellites beam one to the other to create the larger network. The Multi-Dimensional Leader is the beam between the satellites."

— M. Cubas

Multi-Dimensional Excellence includes identifying these abilities:

Fish, flesh or fowl? — What do you stand for?

Establish clear roles and rules for the participants.

With clarity of purpose your people will follow you anywhere. They are seeking a reliable, unwavering source of consistency in an unstable world.

Clearly broadcast the purpose and expected benefits to each employee.

Stimulate an environment where success happens constantly. It becomes contagious. Provide recognition (award, gift, media attention) for team members and supporters. Celebrate events at the end of the project so all can share. Draw for an exceptional prize to up the ante; it creates excitement, it's fun, and they want to keep doing it! It's cheaper than forced "motivation" and short-term fixes.

Offer strategic transitions, adaptation and modification for the existing company culture. Follow-up. Be candid about what worked and what didn't. Learn from it.

Define and apply Entrepreneurial Energy.™ Entrepreneurs have the uncanny ability to breathe life and wonder into ideas. We can apply that in our professional and personal lives.

Deliver a copy of the company's "Fieldbook," the ways "we do business here."

Strategize and encourage visionary and values-driven leadership in others who share your core values. You won't have to waste energy "watching your back" with these team members.

Casting Call™ — Audition for Excellence taps talent at its root. Your clear definitions of purpose and goals lure the appropriate candidate for the position.

Here are suggestions to stimulate your thinking:
- Compile a quarterly membership project of 'real-world' case studies in which participants can apply their expertise — marketing, business planning, finance, and international business development.
- Assist the group in developing realistic post-graduate expectations with real business examples gathered during a "scavenger hunt" during which they have to contact businesses for information.
- Keep research on file for future team members' reference. Reduce the learning curve.
    — Initiate a company recycling program.
    — Publish the results of savings, findings, impacts.
    — It builds hands-on experience for resumés
    — Develops and steers commitment.
    — Creates a revenue stream and working project model for future study.
- Explore the international business process. Learn a global view of your business from exchange team members to shorten the learning curve:
    — Build on their contacts — Use the internet to contact people in other countries in similar fields.
    — Get their feedback of how your products and services could work for them.
    — Ask how they can provide contacts and colleagues for future feedback.
- Set up a chat group with smartgroups.com or yahoogroups.com
    — Tariffs
    — Customs (handout)
    — Letters of credit

— Banking
— Currency exchange
— Cultural integration Global Readiness™
- Conduct round-table events with business people — find out what their customers, vendors are seeking
- Encourage ways to fuel enthusiasm, team building involvement activities like off-site, interactive challenges for depth not competition.
- Classy events like a masked gala raise esteem while encouraging creativity. Historic/theme dress, historical beginnings related to your industry, talent shows pool talent and bring out the best in people.
- Sponsor community sporting events — school/public as proposed by the employees, their children's teams, appropriate causes.
- Consistently sponsor a community program that relates to your vision like Camp CEO for 9-12th grade girls to learn about business, Make-A-Wish Foundation to fulfill dreams to gravely ill children, Habitat for Humanity that rewards sweat equity and builds pride.

Personal Power and Vision
Excerpt from <u>Casting Call</u>™ Hiring Strategy

A Day in the Life of an Organization
A Sample Model

This method can be applied in any industry. The premise of Casting Call is to have candidates prove themselves through demonstrating their abilities rather than listing tasks and activities. The focus is on the traits and talents required for the optimum person to fill a role and function.

Group Interview Activity: (5 minutes individually then 5 minutes in group to compare.)

- List the qualities of leadership necessary for the next decade?
- Demonstrate how membership in this company can support the development of these qualities.

Group:
1. Select a community leader as a recipient of a special award who embodies your vision of leadership.
2. Clearly state what impression s/he creates.

Group:
Sanity check for success —
1. What you think about determines how you pursue your life.
2. Why did you attend school?
3. What do you need to know about this company to make all the pieces work harmoniously?
4. Membership in an organization has to support goals and be productive with your time. How can this company best support your goals?

As you see, Multi-Dimensional Excellence is simple yet multifaceted. It is centered on being rather than doing. It touches all sensory aspects of the human experience — compassion, energy, exchange, vitality, emotion, feelings, action. The authenticity comes from the involvement and participation rather than remote viewing and talking that goes on in most organizations.

Essential skills are active listening, encourage others to take risks, set clear boundaries based on decency, and room to make mistakes. Like attracts like. We're counting on it, to attract more of the same.

The Multi-Dimensional Leader is present at every level of the organization and serves as the congealing factor that seals it all together. The Multi-Dimensional Leader is the ideal we all think of when we want to cheer for someone, stand for an ovation, and link our hopes to a human hero for a productive and enriched future.

About Michelle Cubas

*M*ichelle Cubas is an enterprise coach, business author and national public speaker. Her expertise is reflected in her Multi-Dimensional Leadership programs. Michelle's advanced business practice focuses on contemporary business issues such as Currency of the New Economy and its impact, business literacy, communication effectiveness and its relationship to management styles, and the renewed role of personal responsibility and self-reliance in today's volatile business climate. Michelle knows the value of multi-dimensional communication. Her open style and mentoring approach work together for an optimum learning experience for her keynote and seminar audiences. As a business coach hired by corporations and business owners, Michelle's coaching expertise brings a real-world perspective and applications to multi-generational marketing and sales matters. Also, Michelle offers publishing consulting through Pen Ultimate Publishing Company, a platform for business experts who want their works published.

Contact Information:
Michelle Cubas
Positive Potentials, LLC
7120 E. Sixth Avenue, Suite 21
Scottsdale, AZ 85251
Phone: (480) 922-9699
Fax: (480) 663-6851
E-mail: MCubas@PositivePotentials.com
Website: www.PositivePotentials.com

THE
LANGUAGE OF LEADERSHIP

by Jim Vance

We hear it in times of crisis, in times of mourning, and in times of creation and renewal. It has a lasting quality that can reach across the centuries and span the distance between human hearts. The experience of magnetic or powerfully attractive communication is palpable. It has the ability to touch us, to move and motivate us, and to infuse us with an energy that was somehow missing prior to the experience. When we stand in the presence of a person who consciously or unconsciously practices it, we can walk away inspired. When we watch its duplication on film, when actors assume the charismatic qualities of those who move us, we feel it. But what is it? What enables one leader to communicate magnetically, while another fails to lead or falls back on the meager tools of force? What is it about a communicator and communication that evokes willing collaboration, as opposed to resistance or passive conformity? In the next few pages, we will answer these questions by exploring the language of leadership. We will look at its underlying principles and their application. We will look at the *how* and *what* of this type of communication.

The *how* of the language of leadership is this thing called magnetism. When we think of truly magnetic people — whether they be politicians, business leaders, religious leaders, singers, salespeople, or that person with a certain sparkle in your neighborhood — there is something about these people that sets them apart from the average. Magnetic leaders show an aura of confidence backed by a resonant emotional feeling that harmonizes with the words of a message. They mean what they say. A singer who sings of love becomes magnetic when he feels genuine love in the midst of the song. The words of love come alive. A leader who speaks of compassion and who feels it with genuine strength when delivering a message can move our souls. A conversation with a child in which one listens from the heart and provides the gentle self-disclosure that says, "*I've been there*," can change a life.

A leader has been down the road he is inviting you to take. In order to show the way, the leader must *know* the way. As with anything we come to know in life, a leader's way becomes known by direct experience or by intuitive foresight. There are only two ways to go down the road. The first is to make a physical journey, to go down the road and study the path. The leader sees its cracks, potholes, and crevasses, and knows where they are. This leader returns to us and imparts his knowledge of the path, backed by the grounded credibility of experience. He simplifies the journey of those who follow. This leader has learned every inch of the path and can rely on his knowledge of the familiar to address the unexpected. Through his work, study, and experience, he has become a master of the terrain.

The second way to go down the road is to make a mental journey. The leader intuits or visualizes a path different from the one shown by current conditions. This leader takes people to new places on an untraveled path. This intuitive or creative leader sees a positive future and presents it to others with language that describes the new path. This leader speaks of purpose, possibility, deliverance, gratitude, and the creation of new realities. These are persons who have a vision of what life can be like, can convince others of the efficacy of that vision, and can venture forth with the aid of the collective action of those they inspire. These leaders can literally lift us out of situations that shrink our humanity and take us to new, more ennobling levels of competence, confidence, and self-expression that go beyond the mundane, beyond the fear of loss and failure.

The what of the language of leadership is the message that invites us down the road. There are several principles that help make this message powerfully attractive.

- The magnetic leader communicates information about the road,

and his feelings about the road, in language that people understand.
- The leader must ensure that there is not too great a gap between the description of the road and what people believe they can handle through their own action.
- The leader must communicate in language that inspires.
- The leader must take our minds off of the obstacles of fear, doubt, and contrary goals that lie along the path, and imbue them instead with possibility and potentiality.
- The leader must embody an emotional state that people want to experience.
- The leader must build momentum through the demonstration of progress and by setting up a motivating structure.
- Finally, the magnetic leader must demonstrate visible commitment to the purpose behind the required action.

The Roman statesman Seneca once stated, "When one comes to the top of the hill, the way is easy, even though it is difficult." Nowhere is this more true than when communicating effectively with others. To do so, a leader must communicate in language that people understand. This process goes far beyond using uncomplicated words to communicate a message. It is the demonstration of the ability to set one's perspective aside and communicate with others in words and descriptions they are familiar with. The words a person uses reflect the climate of attitudes, beliefs, truths, and opinions that an individual holds as valid with regard to the way the world works. A leader understands this, and communicates from the point of view (or worldview) of the listener. The leader takes a top-of-the-hill perspective that enables him to see another perspective without sacrificing his self-concept, and without making the other person's perspective wrong.

We can look at this idea of communicating from another angle by stepping back in time to the tragic events of September 11. Let's give ourselves some geographic distance from those events and travel some 10,000 miles across the globe to a tiny, remote village in Kenya, the home of the Masai people. Multistory buildings are a foreign concept in this part of the world where images of trees and giraffes are the tallest things to mark the horizon. Television does not exist here, and radio contact with the outside world is limited. The Masai in this remote area were largely bypassed by the events of September 11.

To understand the Masai, it is necessary to understand that they still live much as they did 3,000 years ago, at the dawn of the Iron Age. The Masai are herdsmen who live in huts made of mud, dung, and sticks. They raise and protect cattle, their source of life in the African grassland. They have no written language; their traditions are oral traditions. These are a people who never fell victim to slavery. When a Masai was captured, he would pine away and die before reaching the slave port. A British naturalist who lived with the Masai had this to say: "They are an intelligent and truthful people. A grown Masai will not steal or lie. He may refuse to answer a question, but when he gives you his word, he can be depended upon."

The Masai are a warrior people. When a boy reaches his late teens, and it is an approximate thing because the Masai do not keep chronological track of their age, he is initiated into warriorhood and wears his hair in long woven locks that are dyed red with local clay. Warriors travel in pairs, because the Masai believe that no matter how brave a man you are, two brave men are better. When a Masai kills the king of beasts, a lion, he is treated with greater respect and adulation than any football star in this country ever received.

When a warrior turns about thirty, the elders of the tribe, in an elaborate ceremony, spit mouthfuls of milk and honey — symbols of health and prosperity — on the man, saying: "Now you are an elder. Put your weapons aside, and use your head and your wisdom instead." The time for marriage and children has begun.

While we can be moved by the mythic nature and seeming simplicity of the Masai, the old ways are changing. Electricity has recently reached Masai villages. Some Masai are attending college at universities in the US. One such student is now attending Stanford University. When this student, Kimeli Naiyomah, recently returned to his village, he found that his people had only a vague notion of the events of September 11th. The warrior chief told him, "I just never heard about it."

In the oral tradition that the Masai use, Kimelli Nayoma sat down with his people and told stories of the events of September 11. The Masai were stunned. They felt deep sadness. They wanted to do something — and they did do something. They contacted the US embassy, and on a warm Sunday in June, in a solemn ceremony in a grassy clearing, the Masai blessed fourteen of their cattle and gave them to the people of the United States.

When there is so much chronological and geographic distance between cultures, it is easy to see that in order to communicate a message from a society effectively, one must communicate in language that the receivers of the message understand. It's also easy to see that a genuine expression from the heart reaches across cultures and requires no explanation. The heartfelt emotions of compassion, generosity, and gratitude require no translation. Neither do their manifestations: tears, laughter, and unaffected warmth and sincerity. We get the message — in this case, so much so that Kimelli Naiyomah, the student, has been literally deluged with the attempts of American citizens to convey gratitude.

The juxtaposition of words, actions, and feelings in language that the listener understands is a potent force. It bridges time and distance. It is easy to see. Not so easy to see is the fact that when we communicate with a stranger, neighbor, coworker, associate or friend, this person may be 10,000 miles away from us with regard to our separate perspectives in certain areas. To reach people, a leader must begin with the assumption of a large difference in perspective. He must speak, perhaps, of a large hut with many levels that can hold the population of one hundred villages. He must set aside his own worldview, and enter the worldview of another, and communicate with him there in small ways. When this is done, magic begins to happen.

The magnetic leader goes beyond simply informing. He must use words, symbols, and metaphors, for which people already understand the intended meaning. The leader's words and actions say: "I value you, I am in many ways like you, and I am going to take you to a better place." Leaders use words that have an emotional connection with would-be followers. When Winston Churchill became Prime Minister of Britain following the resignation of Chamberlain during the World War

II invasion of Holland and Belgium, he began his leadership by saying, "I have nothing to offer you but blood, toil, tears, and sweat." All of these words connect with us in a visceral way. We know their meaning. These are potent words, and with them, Churchill offered the very things that he would expect from his countrymen.

Magnetic leaders not only communicate in language we understand, they appeal to our sense of possibility. They do this by ensuring that there is not too great a leap gap between the perceived requirements of the road and the perception that those that are being led have of their abilities to make meaningful progress down that road. Ultimately it is the meaning that we give words and circumstances that motivates us. In our work, it is easy to see that the vast majority of people would rather work on a meaningful task than a meaningless task. Magnetic leaders control the meaning of events. The leader looks for meanings that not only inspire, or breathe life into us, but also translate a current situation into a situation that we can handle. If, on September 12, 2001, you had asked any single group of people to begin to heal the hurt of the terrorist attack on New York City, you would likely have been met with looks of shock and dismay. But give a group of construction workers the goal of having the offices of the outer ring of the damaged Pentagon back in use before the anniversary of the disaster, and provide them with evidence that in healing the building, they are helping to heal the nation, then the dedication and commitment that follows is phenomenal. This is what happened with the Pentagon repair project. The construction crew was so focused on completing the project that when offered much-needed time off, which would have been gladly accepted in other circumstances, they protested and asked to continue working. The people who were part of this effort, were part of something significant — a meaningful event that may well have defined many lives.

Churchill is an excellent example of the language of leadership and its inspirational qualities. In times of crisis, we often forget our abilities, our accomplishments, and our potential. It is the leader's job to help us remember. It is the leader's job to take the events of the day and sort them into a meaning that inspires us. Churchill's statement regarding Hitler ("Who does he think we are? We have not journeyed across the centuries, across the oceans, across the mountains, across the prairies, because we are made of sugar candy.") drew upon such potential. In short order, his words turned what could have been Britain's darkest hour into its finest hour. Here was leadership that ventured down an untraveled path and refused to be cowed by the apparent strength of the German war machine.

Churchill was a man who had tried and failed, who had been tested and was found wanting, whose prescient nature went unheeded, and who, in the 1930's found himself in the political nether world of minor roles. To support himself, he spent those years writing, and his work, Marlborough: His Life and Times, remains a wisdom-laden treatise on leadership. Churchill's study of history made him aware of the rocks and crevasses along the path of appeasement. He was well aware that trusting a tyrant who consistently did not keep his word would continue to have unfortunate consequences. In this respect, Churchill had become a master of terrain. He expressed his knowledge of it when he said, as he began to prepare his nation for the coming war with Germany, "We have to assume the burden of the most thankless tasks, and in undertaking them, be scoffed at, criticized, and opposed from every quarter."

A look at history shows the overwhelming nature of Hitler's advance on Europe. On May 10, 1940 — the day Churchill assumed the role as Prime Minister — Hitler's armies had just invaded Holland, spearheaded by some nine armored divisions with about 400 vehicles each. When the King of Belgium appealed for help, the British sent the core of their army with 400,000 troops and their best weapons to support their ally. In the face of the German onslaught, he directed a retreat of British forces to the Port of Dunkirk on the Franco-Belgian border. On May 28, 1940, Belgium's king surrendered his army of 500,000 men to the Germans, effectively leaving a thirty-mile flank of the British forces open to attack. Now in desperate retreat, some 400,000 British and French troops poured into this allied stronghold, and fortifications were put in place to hold out as long as possible. Some two weeks into his leadership, Churchill recognized that France would quickly fall. He realized that, in order for his nation to have heart when the world appeared heartless, there must be a sense of progress toward the goal of freedom rather than a sense of progressive failure. He gave the painful order to save the British airforce for the defense of England, rather than lose it in the defeat of France.

Churchill directed an evacuation, under the code name Operation Dynamo, hoping to rescue 45,000 men. He put his faith in Vice Admiral Bertram Ramsey by giving him full authority to conduct the evacuation, in spite of the fact that Ramsey was open to ideas that had been dismissed as ridiculous by top brass. After evacuation efforts by military vessels showed that it would take weeks to pull out the allied forces, time that the British did not have in the face of the advancing German army, Ramsey quickly changed tactics. The Admiralty called on the owner of a boatyard and gave the directive to gather every private seaworthy vessel and every willing owner that could be found, have them sail some 40 miles to the beaches at Dunkirk, and begin to ferry soldiers to waiting destroyers and transports. Scarcely a man refused the call. No one forced them to go. They went willingly. With the British airforce working valiantly to keep German bombers at bay, the evacuation began to succeed. Over the course of the next seven days, an unlikely collection of hundreds of tugboats, yachts, barges, fishing vessels, tour craft, and pleasure boats, frequently captained by civilians, many in their yachting smart jackets, under constant attack from the Germans, rescued 338,000 men. The British effectively pulled off one of the greatest military feats of all time.

When presenting a report to the House of Commons at the conclusion of Operation Dynamo, Churchill said: "We shall go on to the end . . . we shall fight with growing confidence and growing strength in the air . . . we shall fight on the beaches, we shall fight on the landing grounds, we shall fight in the fields and in the streets, we shall fight in the hills; we shall never surrender . . ." However, he also tempered his remarks with the realism of: "We must be careful not to assign to this deliverance the attributes of victory. Wars are not won by evacuations."

Magnetic leaders use action and language that inspire. They assess the present and set in motion the steps that harmonize with their vision of the future. Inspiration is what calls us forth to a meaning that transcends a hopeless or negative future. It recalls to our attention our abilities and capabilities that we may for the moment have forgotten about. It is about using language that not only gives the events of our world an empowering, compelling meaning, but taps into the very fabric of who we are and invites us to become more.

The magnetic leader imbues the mind with possibility and potentiality. Such a leader sees a compelling future despite evidence to the contrary. It is human nature to focus on the collective emotion of our society. Influenced by news reports that are often filled with tales of woe, we can fall prey to the human condition of propensity for focusing on what is not working, and a current situation that disempowers us. Because of our human nature, we distort, delete, and generalize the body of information to which we are exposed to give it meaning. A leader's job is to refocus our thinking on what we have left out, so that the meaning of events can be reinterpreted in a way that empowers us. It is easy to adopt an apocalyptic posture in the face of terrorism, man's inhumanity to man, or a stock market crash. It is another matter to wake up to the fact that your entire heritage has gotten you to this point. It is another matter to realize that your ancestors, whose legacy you carry, have collectively survived such travails with determination and resolve. It is another matter to realize that once inspired, we are bigger, stronger, and more durable than the malaise of the moment. Yes, you have failings as well as strengths, but even in your failings you can find strengths. It is your strengths that will pull you through. By keeping on keeping on, this, too, shall be overcome.

Churchill brought out in the British people the qualities of uncommon valor, good humor, self-sacrifice, steadfastness in the face of overwhelming odds, and statesmanship in the face of victory. It is no small coincidence that Churchill embodied the very qualities and characteristics his leadership brought out in others. He practiced both types of leadership, and his reputation, a consequence of the alignment of words, feelings, and actions, has not diminished with time. Regardless of what you may think of the class structures and imperialism of which he was a part, he is regarded as England's greatest statesman of the 20th century.

The powerfully attractive communicator embodies an emotional state that people want to experience and don't know how to access at the moment. Einstein is often quoted as saying that a problem cannot be solved by the same level of thinking that created it. Magnetic leaders go a step further. They consciously or unconsciously recognize that a problem cannot be overcome with the same level of feeling that created it.

Emotions are contagious, and magnetic leaders use their very being to embody the emotional antidote to the current situation. Would you rather follow a fearful or a confident person into the face of uncertain outcome? Would you rather follow someone who visibly and emotionally cares for what you value, or someone who wants success regardless of price? Churchill embodied courage, steadfastness, good humor, and resilience — the antidote to the fear, despair, defeat, and inaction that could have been the response to the apparent momentum of the German onslaught. In the face of the bombing of Britain, he spent as much time as possible among the British people. He was a contagious source of inspiration to those who were in his presence. His words and actions, the language of his leadership, became purposeful when they were backed by heartfelt emotions that communicated a consistent message.

The magnetic leader realizes that stepped-up emotion and inspiring words have impact that all too often fail to motivate when the leader is absent. The leader must build a structure that builds on the momentum catalyzed by his communication. It is all too easy for followers to focus on the evidence around them that belies the vision of the future. Like a pot of boiling water, to which energy must be continually added to keep it boiling, the leader must set up a system to infuse his followers with energy. He must set up a system that attracts followers with the flame of inspiration. This system keeps the pot boiling and provides followers with the matches and kindling necessary to sustain their smaller fires. It is the fire in the hearts of individual followers that serves to keep progress alive.

Magnetic leaders set up this system with knowledge of effective motivation. They know that people are motivated when they work on a meaningful goal and are presented with evidence of meaningful progress. Imagine a situation in which you were asked to work on a goal that did not matter to you. Imagine that in working toward that goal, there was no feedback to let you know how well you were doing, and that any feedback you did get was negative. This prescription for apathy is what the language of leadership avoids. Magnetic leaders ensure that their followers are aware of successes and progress, and that they have the freedom to use their strengths to overcome setbacks. These leaders communicate progress to build momentum, a sense of possibility, and accomplishment. They use their words and emotions to show followers that their individual actions are making a contribution to the collective whole. They declare as Churchill did regarding his country's beleaguered airforce, "Never in the field of human conflict has so much been owed by so many to so few." They know that in beginning an endeavor, often the leader's appreciation is often the only visible sign of progress.

To increase your ability to speak the powerfully attractive language of leadership, you must:

- Study, and become a master of your terrain. Discover a road that will enoble the spirit, that when traversed will cause people to be, do, and become more of themselves.
- Communicate information about the road in language that is meaningful to your followers.
- Tell your followers how their individual actions make a positive difference, and provide feedback as an indicator of progress. Set up communication and feedback systems that give clear indications of progress.
- Watch your emotions. If you do not come from a place of courage, dedication, confidence, respect, and gratitude, you cannot inspire these attitudes in others. Embody the emotions and actions that will be necessary to actualize the goal.
- Set up communication and feedback systems that give clear indications of progress.

Believe in what you are doing, and mean what you say. Perhaps one day, if you are very lucky, a follower will come back to you and say, "Thanks, you made a difference in my life." In that fortunate time, you will see a deeper meaning; you will see the consequences of the how and what of your leadership.

About Jim Vance

*J*im Vance is president of Advanced Business Resources, a firm that specializes in people management and human interaction training. Jim is a former human resource and training director who transitioned from a successful career in engineering to human resources and then to speaking and consulting. With over fifteen years experience in people management, project management, and talent acquisition, Jim brings balance and perspective to the critical issues of workplace communication, employment practice, and getting things done through others. A sought-after speaker who has delivered programs to business audiences in thirty-eight states, Jim's dynamic presentation style and real-world course materials help participants learn, relate the learning to their life wisdom, and experience the benefit of applying new behaviors in the workplace context.

Contact Information:
Jim Vance
Advanced Business Resources
4912 Yoakum Boulevard
Houston, TX 77006
Phone: (713) 527-8893
Email: jim@abr-training.com
Website: www.abr-training.com

Intuitive Leadership: Transformation and Change from the "Insight" Out

by Edie Raether, M.S., CSP

*The success of the actions of great men
depends more upon the purity of their hearts than
upon the means of their actions.*

— Vedas

When you lead, will they follow? You obviously cannot be a leader if you have no followers. Leadership is the ability to inspire others into goal-oriented and focused action, guided by a consensual vision and driven by a purposeful mission. It is facilitating change from the "insight out" out to create a compassionate culture and team synergy for optimal performance and the fulfillment of personal and organizational goals. While traditional leadership gave power to those of position and authority, today's savvy workforce no longer concedes to blind obedience. The only real leadership will come from those who inspire, which has been the most profound leadership of the past as well. Certainly leaders such as Martin Luther King, Abraham Lincoln, Ghandi and Golda Meier have known the power of intuition and inspiration long before a slew of books on leadership hit the marketplace. The definition for the word inspire is to fill with noble or reverent emotion, to stimulate creativity or action, to stimulate the mind or emotions to a high level. There is no reference to control or manage, but rather to stimulate.

Inspiring leaders understand the essence of internal motivation, which is based on a personal and team purpose and shared goals and vision which create a powerful synergy. Certainly the Chicago Bulls demonstrated the magic of synergy when Jordan and Jackson gave roots to a team that broke most NBA basketball records. W. Edwards Deming introduced a higher level of excellence and the concept of TQM, total quality management, by providing opportunities and an environment that allowed people to enjoy their work while setting high expectations for performance, which increased the workers' self-esteem and personal job satisfaction. Team solutions that work are those developed by the team itself, and thus employee involvement and team participation revolutionized our management protocol with acknowledgment of the interdependence of humankind. How we implement that acquired knowledge will thus depend on the awareness and personal integrity of leaders. The Harvard Business School has recently reported that "awareness" is the most important quality to be found in today's leaders.

The communication network of an organization may be likened to the interdependence of the nervous system in the human body, for information must flow to the brain for actions to be coordinated and supportive of the integrity of the whole. It's all about understanding systems, which are totally dependent upon information networks. The human body illustrates the interdependence of systems, for information must flow to the brain for actions to be coordinated and supportive of the integrity of the whole. A person who is intoxicated disrupts his internal information system and thus loses the ability to coordinate its parts and walk effectively. If we lose one of our senses, such as sight or hearing, we are functioning at a distinct disadvantage. Think of a blind person crossing the street in traffic. Likewise, an organization which loses sight of changes in the marketplace will have difficulties staying in business. The interconnectedness of all parts of the body to mission control or command central, the brain, is another similarity between the human body and social organizations and corporate cultures. If there is an injury to any part of your body, all attention is immediately directed to that area which has instant demands. Not only is the mind aware of the information and energy of its own quantum field, but because human consciousness is infinitely flexible through this wonderful nervous system, you are able to consciously change the informational content that gives rise to your physical body. You can consciously change the energy and informational content of your own quantum mechanical body, and therefore influence the energy and informational content of your extended environment, your world — and cause things to manifest in it. This conscious change is brought about by the two qualities inherent in consciousness: attention and intention. Whatever you put your attention on will grow stronger in your life. Whatever you take your attention away from will wither, disintegrate, and disappear. Intention, on the other hand, triggers energy and information. Intention organizes its own fulfillment. The quality of intention on the object of attention will orchestrate an infinity of space-time events to bring about the outcome intended, provided one follows the other spiritual laws of success. Inherent in every intention and desire are the mechanics for their fulfillment. Intention and desire in the field of pure potentiality have infinite organizing power. And when we introduce an intention in the fertile ground of pure potentiality, we put the infinite organizing power to work for us.

An organization has a "personality" just like a person. Leaders must treat their organizations like the living organisms that they are. Although the body can continue to function with injured limbs, when certain organs such as the heart or lungs lose function, one is totally disabled. Very similarly, the leadership is the heart of that organization.

Leaders of the future will need to focus on managing minds and transforming mindsets. I call it MindShift, which is the facilitation of change from the "insight out," which can only be accomplished through awareness and understanding, not by force, intimidation, or by overpowering. Goals must be holistic and always for the "greater good." Leaders must redefine themselves as servants rather than as managers, and as orchestrators of an interdependent matrix of unique people and perceptions. As leaders challenge existing mindsets and allow their team members to explore new realities, innovation and creativity are ignited. It is innovation and creativity that will propel companies of the future, as they are the key ingredients for organizational and corporate survival. Our intuitive intelligence is a sensory feedback system that unleashes the enlightened "ahas" which are a catalyst to innovation and creativity. Twenty first century leadership will thus require one to orchestrate an environment, which will unleash the Power Zone, the other 90 percent of untapped potential, in all team members.

Future leaders will need to become masters of the mind. They will teach people how to rewire their brainware and thus reprogram their minds for sustained peak performance. It will include properly selecting the right person for the right job or task so that natural skills and abilities are utilized for maximum benefit and people are in personal and team alignment, exercising the power of "flow." Flow moves people to do their best work, no matter what work they do. Flow blossoms when our skills are fully engaged and then some. The challenge absorbs us so much we lose ourselves in our work, becoming so totally concentrated we may feel "out of time." It is a pleasurable state in which we seem to handle everything effortlessly and with ease. Athletes refer to it as the Zone, a special place where their performance is exceptional and consistent, automatic and flowing. An Olympic figure skater described it as "the performance where everything clicks. It's very fun to be in. No worries are present." Michael Jordan so eloquently demonstrates flow when he shoots a 3-pointer with a split second on the clock in a triple overtime. Wynton Marsalis is one with his horn to produce music that awakens the spirit and Tiger Woods illustrates flow when he is in the Zone. Most recently, Sarah Hughes demonstrated flow at the 2002 Olympics with her breathtaking performance in the women's figure skating events. When she approached the ice, she said quietly to herself, "I'm going to have fun" — a key component of flow.

People in flow often make the difficult look easy, an external appearance that mirrors what is happening in their brain. Flow poses a neural paradox: We can be engaged in an exceptionally demanding task, and yet our brain is operating with a minimal level of activity or expenditure of energy. The reason seems to be that when we are bored and apathetic, or frenzied with anxiety, our brain activity is diffused: the brain itself is at a high level of activation, albeit poorly focused, with brain cells firing in far-flung and irrelevant ways. But during flow, the brain appears efficient and precise in its pattern of firing. The result is an overall lowering of cortical arousal, even though the person may be engaged in an extremely challenging task.

Mihalyi Csikzentmihalyi, the University of Chicago psychologist who pioneered the study of flow, outfitted 107 people in positions from management and engineering to the assembly line with a beeper that periodically reminded them to note what they were doing and how they felt. The results were surprising. They reported, on average, being in flow about half the time while on the job, and less than twenty percent of the time during their leisure hours. The most common emotional state reported during leisure time was apathy!

But there was also a wide variation in just how much of the time people were in flow at work. Those with complex, challenging jobs, who had more flexibility in how they approached each task, were most likely to be in flow. Managers and engineers had more flow time than those in routine jobs. More control means more opportunity to maximize flow. Control can take many forms, even putting something off until the last minute as a way to up the challenge, creating a pressured "rush" period that adds adrenaline to an otherwise easy task. Great performers learn to quiet their brains and create a state of quiet alertness in they are which mentally relaxed but 100 percent focused on the task or activity in which they are engaged. Psychologist Michael Posner of the University of Oregon used a new technology called PET scanning to look at the brain activity of people who were paying attention to a new task. When they tried the task for the first time, their blood flow increased in the brain. But as they had more practice with the task, the blood flow and brain electrical activity decreased.

For top performers, there is an especially tight calibration of flow and task; flow occurs in the work that is most critical to their goals and productivity, rather than in fascinating diversions or irrelevancies. For the stars, excellence and pleasure in work are one and the same.

To achieve team or group flow, there must be a strong challenge or worthy mission. The vice president of space launch systems at Lockheed Martin said, " One of the reasons group goals often fail is they're too materialistic. I look for super-ordinary goals big enough that the whole group can get behind them. Such work has compelling meaning and motivation: working toward something monumental deserves everyone's best effort."

The late Nobel Prize-winning physicist Prichard Feynman remembered how differently people worked on the Manhattan Project before and after they knew what their effort was for. Originally, strict security meant the whole team was kept in the dark, so they often worked slowly, and not always very well. Then Feynman convinced Robert Oppenheimer to tell the team of technicians what they were actually working on. It was during the darkest days of World War II, and their project was a weapon that might stop the Axis enemy who were at the time ascendant. From that point on, Feynman recalled, "complete transformation. They began to invent ways of doing it better." He calculated that their work went ten times as fast after they understood the goal.

Flow accelerates when we are challenged and our skills are fully engaged to stretch us. No matter how routine the task, flow stimulates people to do their best work. Flow is the ultimate motivator. It is built into the work we love to do and is its own internal reward. Motive and emotion share the same Latin root, motere, "to move." It is thus our emotions that fuel our motivations and behaviors. Computers lack the guide force that emotions and motivations allow us. Many people may unconsciously procrastinate on projects and then create a last minute "rush" to create a challenge and surge of adrenalin. In fact, it may be considered an internal drug addiction, similar to the natural "high" produced by endorphins. This internal stage of pleasure is the essence of self- motivation.

Intuitive leadership is about integrating and implementing the benefits of flow into the workplace. It is about hiring the right person for the right job, or correcting situations where misalignment is obvious. Visionary leadership has implicit limitations as it takes much more than a leader with a vision. The Harvard Business School reports that the number one quality in leadership is awareness. Mechanical mindsets resist awareness. The robot style of leadership, which operates on automatic programming, usually forces solutions that fit certain mindsets rather than shape solutions that fit the demands of the problem. John Gardner states "a society whose maturing consists simply of acquiring more firmly established ways of doing things is headed for the graveyard — even if it learns to do these things with greater and greater skill. In the ever-renewing society, what matures is a system or framework within which continuous innovation, renewal and rebirth can occur." Thus, the role of leaders will now be focused on facilitating and nurturing an open and creative mindset, which I refer to as MindShift.

Since all competing organizations offer similar products for a matching price, duplicate guarantees and customer service, or more accurately, a customer service department, the creativity and innovation of each employee is key to an organization's success and survival. We can no longer merely be reactors to change, but instigators. Reactive leaders are ego-driven and their need for control stifles creative problem- solving. Creative leaders listen to their intuition rather than getting bogged down in analysis paralysis. They are visionary rather than being simply focused on results. They build on strengths and learn from mistakes rather than quickly fire for failure. Their goal is not to impose their vision on others but to support and facilitate visionary thinking in others to create team alignment through a unified commitment to a common mission. Unification assures that we are all pulling in the same direction. The synergy that results from mission-driven alignment empowers teams to do the impossible. An example is the heroic rescue efforts and clean up from the disaster resulting from the terrorist attack of September 11th. In addition to the thousands of lives that were saved from clearly defined unified efforts and also from listening to one's intuition, the clean-up mission was accomplished with less money and in less time than initially projected. It is a reflection of the other 90 percent of untapped potential that we rarely tap into but could utilize for perpetual and consistent peak performance. Unfortunately, out of routine and habit, we continue to function within a comfortable but limited norm of mediocre achievement until our level of motivation and need is enhanced by a crisis. Again, the crisis simply creates a perception of need and conviction, a MindShift, which triggers reserve resources to astounding levels of performance.

Your challenge in providing extraordinary leadership is to sustain such levels of super motivation. The intuitive leader must help develop the imagination and creative thinking of the team. He or she must have each team member learn to imagine solutions to problems and imagine how they will reach those goals by not only picturing the end goals and results but also the specific actions or stepping stone to the long-term goals. Extraordinary leadership involves educating people on the benefits of practicing visualization and mental/behavioral rehearsal, which trigger neural pathways in the brain, establishing higher levels of excellence as a habit. The ability to "see" pictures in your mind is only part of the power of imagination. Our other senses such as our hearing, taste, smell, touch, and our sixth sense, intuition, all contribute to creating a "feel" of the desired success, which is referred to by scientists as the "kinesthetic" sensation. Our memory of past experiences of success also contributes to getting the "feel" for future performance.

The ultimate tool for personal and team empowerment is found in the art of effective questioning. As Gandhi said, "If you don't ask, you don't get." Questions shape our destiny. The quality of our questions determines the quality of our lives and personal success. Asking questions and listening create a laser focus to one's thoughts and allow people to move in a forward direction in terms of constructive problem solving. Questions increase people's awareness and consciousness, allowing them to break out of routine behaviors and habits and again facilitate a MindShift for more creative, innovative thinking. The process of creative thinking is oftentimes more important than the answer or solution. As summarized by James Thurber, "It is better to know some of the questions than all of the answers." As such, questions bridge the mindset we have to the mindset we desire by stimulating thoughts and possibilities. Albert Einstein emphasized the importance of questions when he said, "The important thing is not to stop questioning."

By encouraging team participation and involvement, people take ownership and responsibility for the results. The more people participate in the change process, the less they resist that change and commit themselves to the solution. The impact of questions also helps people express their wants and needs and also clarifies their understanding of the team or corporate vision and mission. While questions can empower and encourage creative thinking by igniting our intuitive intelligence, questions can also cause defensiveness and distrust. A question like, "what's your problem," may actually increase resistance and become a de-motivator. Obviously, the body language, intonation, inflection and other nonverbals as well as the trust and strength of the relationship will determine how such questions may be perceived. The word "why" is often associated with blaming and accusations as is a finger pointed at you.

When asking questions it is also important to sequence them properly for optimal mind empowerment. You must first ask "what" questions, which stimulate visionary, big-picture thinking. Donald Trump says, "If you're going to think anyhow, you might as well think big." Then, too, vision and mission tend to inspire and rekindle the human spirit and unleash one's Power Zone, the other 90 percent. Vision and mission triggers one's intuitive intelligence and inner genius and resourcefulness. "Don't tell people how to do things. Tell them what to do and let them surprise you with their results," according to WWII General George Patton. The "why" questions serve a purpose in that they give people an understanding and reason for the desired accomplishment and achieved goal. This is an especially strong motivator for left-brain, logical, linear thinkers. They need to see a strong rationale for any activity to deserve their attention. Right-brain people, on the other hand, are quite excited and convinced by the possibilities presented by the big picture. The "how" questions also serve a purpose in that they create concrete steps and action plans to execute and put all the details in place to make it happen. We do need all three, but only in that order. To discuss how we are going to execute a plan that has no blueprint is like driving a car with no place to go. It has no excitement, no purpose or meaning, and thus we would probably elect to just take a walk instead. Since the level of growth of the team members tends not to supersede the growth of the team leader, the pivotal point of the organization is contingent upon your intention and the motive behind your actions and aspirations.

The model of transformational leadership, rather than traditional management, requires one who is charismatic, inspires by modeling enthusiasm, and arouses excitement, emotions and commitment to a shared vision, mission, and valued identity. "We are family" might be an appropriate motto. Beyond the carrot and stick, pay and promotions, inspirational leadership compels one to action and mobilizes and unifies the team, creating a team synergy, which is a one-or two-way exchange of ideas and collaboration, a much more effective way of idea development than spawning nuggets of thought by oneself. Fresh ideas strengthen promising solutions.

John Kotter, a Harvard Business School leadership expert, cites the difference between "management" and "leadership." He refers to management as the system of keeping things orderly, non chaotic, and productive. Leadership is referred to as the effective handling of changes of our times. "Motivation and inspiration energize people, not by pushing them in the right direction as control mechanisms but by satisfying basic human needs for achievement, a sense of belonging, a feeling of control over one's life, and the ability to live up to one's ideals. Such feelings touch us deeply and elicit a powerful response." Daniel Goleman refers to leadership of this kind as an emotional craft. However, destructive emotions also spread like wildfire and demoralize the group. Birgitta Wistrand uses the term "emotional incontinence" for the leakage of destructive emotions from the top down. The charismatic, versus the manipulative leader, is sincere, emotionally convincing and inspiring due to the authenticity, integrity and congruency conveyed when one speaks from the heart. Your body doesn't lie. Just try to stop sweat! "Mortals can keep no secret. If their lips are silent, they gossip with their fingertips; betrayal forces its way through every pore," said Freud, confirming that emotions cannot be hidden because body language so often contradicts the spoken word.

To be an intuitive leader, you have to think like a genius: you have to break all the rules. Einstein was one of the world's most natural rule breakers, the "James Dean" of science. While rules provide answers, structure, and organization, they limit us from coloring outside the lines where superior solutions often find their roots. Too many rules destroy the human spirit. Rules form naturally, for ideas become rules with repeated use. When a rule rut forms, all conflicting ideas are ignored, limiting innovative and creative thinking. Concept louses up percept. In other words, once we have a belief, conception, or prejudice of how things are, all our perceptions conform to and support that belief system as reality. An example of the limitations of such thinking is illustrated by the numerous murders committed by the DC snipers in the fall of 2002. Police believed the get-away vehicle was a white Astro van, and thus the snipers' blue Chevy Caprice was never suspect, even though they had been stopped and questioned by police a dozen times in just a few weeks. Unfortunately, when we define the answer or solution, we confine and limit our thinking to those perceived beliefs. In the words of Vincent Van Gogh, " Do not quench your inspiration and imagination; do not become a slave of your model." However, there must also be a compelling need for action and a strong motivation for resolution. Ancient Chinese generals had a wonderful motivational tactic. They would put soldiers in a position where retreat was absolutely impossible. They had only two options — fight and prevail, or die. The men fought like dragons. As an intuitive leader, you know that if we can't we must, and if we must we can. How will you effectively incorporate the moral equivalent of such survival tactics for intense focus and optimal performance?

J. Donald Walters describes leadership as intuition guided by common sense and states that a wise leader is more concerned with what is than with the way he or she would like things to be. While guided by intuition, the wise leader must sell his or her convictions with the support of reason, experience, and common sense, which are defined as the willingness to learn from experience. Thus, common sense, while creating a check on intuition, also fosters an openness, which allows the gradual development of intuition. They are essential interdependent concepts, for intuition, in turn, gives wings to the historical roots of past experiences, known as common sense. To demand agreement on the strength of your intuition alone would be a request for blind obedience and submission.

The wise leader is also more concerned with what will work than with getting his mere opinions accepted and more concerned with truth than with merely being thought right. Strong leaders are centered in themselves, but not self-centered. They are at rest inwardly. This inward poise and sense of conviction are the secrets of personal magnetism that distinguishes intuitive leadership from traditional methods based on power by position and authority. Intuitive leadership is more about doing the right thing versus doing things right. It leads people rather than drives them and involves and inspires rather than manipulates. Intuitive leadership is an emotional transfusion of energy, and thus leaders must be in sync with their sources of energy and protect them from depletion. Just as butterflies must spread their wings in the morning sunshine because the scales on their wings are actually solar cells that receive and transform energy to fly, so, too intuitive leaders are transformers of energy, giving wings to their flight team.

About
Edie Raether, M.S., CSP

*E*die Raether is an international speaker, trainer, performance coach and author of Why Cats Don't Bark. *A Fortune 50 favorite, Edie has presented programs to over 3,000 professional associations and corporations such as IBM, Marriott, General Motors, JC Penney, SC Johnson, and Oscar Mayer. As a change strategist, Edie's mind-empowering strategies provide the power tools for mastering change from the "insight" out, helping individuals and organizations bridge the gap between knowing and doing to maximize performance and productivity. Her expertise is in thinking and behavioral styles and in emotional and intuitive intelligence for innovation and creativity in business and management development, increased sales, leadership and life. Her restructuring and recovery programs restore morale after crisis or layoff. President of Performance PLUS, Edie has also been a college professor, psychotherapist, and talk show host with ABC. She is also the recipient of the CSP, Certified Speaking Professional, the National Speakers Association's highest certification, which is held by less than 8% of its membership.*

Contact Information:
Edie Raether
Performance PLUS
4717 Ridge Water Court
Holly Springs, NC 27540
Phone: (919) 557-7900
Fax: (919) 557-7999
E-mail: edie@raether.com
Website: www.raether.com

Extreme Trust: The Magnet of EXTREME Leadership™

by Dave Timmons

What is EXTREME Leadership?™

EXTREME Leadership™ is inspiring performance excellence by finding and using your personal courage to grow people and results. It's the type of leadership that separates great leaders from average managers. *Extreme Leaders* not only produce excellent results, they inspire and develop everyone around them to be the best they can be. Therefore, followers and teammates are strongly attracted to the *magnetism of Extreme Leaders*.

The foundation for this magnetism is rooted in that very important relationship ingredient we call *trust*. This chapter will introduce ways to build, measure, and repair trust, in your quest to become an *Extreme Leader*. Trust is such an important value in the fabric of great leaders, I call it Extreme Trust: The Magnet of *EXTREME Leadership*.™

What is Trust?

TRUST can be defined as *strong belief that some person or thing is honest and can be depended on*. When you think of the great leaders you admire, aren't they always honest and dependable? Extreme Trust is simply the strongest form of trust. It's the kind of trust that attracts people to great leaders. Watson Wyatt Worldwide, an international human capital consulting firm, completed a survey in 2002 of employee trust and confidence in their senior leaders. Out of nearly 13,000 employees surveyed in all industries, Watson Wyatt found fewer than two out of five (39 percent) trust senior leaders at U.S. companies. Dr. Ilene Gochman, author of the survey, states: "Falling levels of employee trust are a major threat to future corporate competitiveness." She goes on to say, "Unless Corporate America can resolve the crisis of confidence among its employees, it has little hope of restoring the trust and confidence of investors that is so crucial in these economic times." Trust is obviously one of the most important elements of the relationship between leaders and their teammates. Can I trust you? That is one of the first questions we ask before we decide to build a relationship with another person. Strangely, it is not a question we often verbalize to the other person but one we constantly ask ourselves silently. The more important the relationship, the more important trust becomes.

Leaders have a greater obligation to be trustworthy because of their circle of influence. When leaders are dishonest and cannot be depended upon, the negative impact is magnified by the number of people affected.

Why Is Trust Important to Leaders?

"Honesty is the single most important factor having a direct bearing on the final success of an individual, corporation, or product."

— Ed McMahon

Leaders are expected to produce results through other people. The very nature of being a leader of others underscores the importance of relationships between leaders and their followers. As mentioned earlier, the more important the relationship, the more important trust becomes.

The level of trust in the leader can dictate whether you are inspired or demoralized, confident or doubtful, courageous or fearful, and enthusiastic or apathetic. People want to follow someone they can trust. The more they trust the leader, the greater their individual effort. The higher their belief in themselves, the more productive they are likely to be.

Extreme Leaders value trust more than anything. They understand how important trust is as a competitive advantage. They not only earn the trust of their teammates, they take it to a level that inspires uncommon behavior and results. They also understand that trust needs to be mutual to be the most effective.

Extreme Leaders must know they can trust their teammates also. Earning a teammate's trust is certainly the first step in creating a strong relationship, but being able to trust teammates as much as they trust the leader is even more powerful. Mutual trust allows people and teams to accomplish more because they depend on each other and believe in each other.

Building Trust

"The truth of the matter is you always know the right thing to do. The hard part is doing it."

— H. Norman Schwarzkopf,
Ret. General, U.S. Army

The process of building trust between a leader and teammates is dynamic and evolutionary. It starts at a certain base level when two or more people begin a relationship. From that moment forward, the level of trust is growing, diminishing, or staying the same. Our trust sensors are always evaluating other people and their behaviors. Are they always honest? Do they keep their promises? Can I always depend on them? Are their behaviors consistent in various situations? Do they walk the talk?

> **Leaders are constantly under a microscope. They are seen and heard by large numbers of people every day. People generally look up to their leaders and, in so doing, pay attention to their every move. Therefore, leaders have multiple opportunities every day to strengthen or weaken their trust bond with their employees. I call these** *moments of trust*. **A moment of trust is created every time a leader makes a** *promise*, **makes a** *mistake*, **or takes an** *action*. **These are the most visible circumstances when teammates tend to evaluate trust in their leaders.**

Leaders build unwavering trust by continually ensuring every moment of trust strengthens their leadership trust bond with their teammates. Let's look at a few suggestions that can strengthen trust when a leader makes a promise, makes a mistake, or takes an action:

Promises

• *Be Aware of Daily Promises:* Leaders unknowingly make promises every day. It may be a simple statement to someone that you will call him or her to set up lunch (but never do) or that you will e-mail a document (but forget). While you may not remember these simple promises, it's important to know that your teammates remember everything and may perceive these simple statements as a form of promise.

A promise is also as simple as a statement that you are going to do something. For example, if you say, "I will take care of it" when a teammate complains about the lack of staffing on busy days, you have made a promise. In his or her mind, you have promised to provide more staffing on busy days. If that doesn't happen, you have weakened a moment of trust. Remember, moments of trust are precious moments that impact the level of trust your teammates have in you as their leader. Learn to be aware of your language and the direct or indirect promises you make on a daily basis.

• *Under-Promise, Over-Deliver:* When you do make a promise of some sort, make sure you are certain you can deliver. The worst thing to do is over-promise and under-deliver. If you under-deliver too often, you will soon be viewed as an undependable leader. Whether you initiate the promise or whether you are asked to do something, make it a point to over-deliver. Leaders who continually do more than expected will be viewed as highly dependable and trustworthy. This is particularly true when promising to do something by a certain deadline. Always give yourself some extra time to be able to deliver on your promise before the deadline.

When making direct or indirect promises, remember to commit to courses of action in which you can exceed expectations when you deliver. Whether you know it or not, your followers are watching, tabulating, and evaluating your record as a promise keeper. Keep your record strong by under-promising and over-delivering.

Mistakes

• *When wrong, quickly admit it:* We all make mistakes and leaders are no exception. Because leaders are held to a higher standard, they must know how to handle those times when they are wrong. Mistakes must be viewed as *learning opportunities during the pursuit of progress.* When leaders make a mistake that is obvious to one or more teammates, it becomes a golden moment of trust. If the leader ignores the mistake and pushes forward, he or she sends a neutral-to-negative message to the team, creating questions about the leader's accountability. On the other hand, quickly admitting a mistake is one of the best ways to capitalize on a moment of trust.

• *Have the Courage to Apologize:* Sometimes a mistake by a leader adversely impacts the lives of one or more of their teammates. In many of these instances, an apology may be in order. Finding the courage to apologize is another character-defining moment for a leader. If an apology is appropriate but not expressed, the leader not only loses some measure of respect but also weakens the level of trust from all affected individuals.

On the other hand, when a leader apologizes, the respect and trust for that leader will rise. I do not subscribe to the old belief that leaders should always present a stern, tough image, and that apologizing only weakens that image and makes a leader soft. Wrong! An apology coming from a leader is one of the most humanizing and honest actions a leader can take. This honesty is yet another way to strengthen, not weaken, a critical moment of trust.

My most memorable example of a leader's acknowledgement of an error in judgment was in 1974, when Richard M. Nixon resigned as President of the United States. Although his role in Watergate was a serious mistake compounded by the cover-up attempt, Nixon took responsibility for his actions and expressed regret to the American people. While he could not justify his actions or save his political career, he was able to salvage some level of respect from the American people. His legacy to this day would have been far different if he had not acknowledged his mistakes.

Have you responded to your leadership mistakes appropriately? Do you have the courage to admit mistakes and apologize to your teammates?

Actions

- *Work Ethic:* A leader's work ethic sends a message of dependability. Leaders that work hard and help their teammates in the trenches will build more trust than those who don't. If a leader says he is going to personally make something happen, and then does it, the trust level will remain strong or rise even further. Conversely, a lazy, uninvolved leader will lose respect quickly and trust will wane.

> *"It is not fair to ask of others what you are not willing to do yourself."*
> — Eleanor Roosevelt

Some of my most memorable leaders in corporate America are those who committed a certain amount of hours each month to work on the frontlines with teammates and customers. While this behavior could be criticized as not making the best use of the leader's time, it galvanized teammates and strengthened trust and respect for the leader. When leaders take these kinds of actions, they demonstrate their interest in and concern for the people they most need to influence.

- *Walk the Talk:* We have previously discussed how important communication is to the role of a leader. Leaders are always communicating in a verbal, non-verbal, or written form. One way to erode trust with your teammates is to talk a big game and not be able to back it up. Followers are keenly aware when a leader's words and actions are incongruent. Those that don't *walk the talk* squander precious moments of trust. Those that do walk the talk are viewed as reliable, dependable, and trustworthy. Extreme Leaders walk their talk!

What message does your work ethic send to your teammates? Do you walk your talk always? Sometimes? Never?

Building Trust among Teammates

Often, there is no issue of trust in the leadership of an organization. Leaders should have proven they can be trusted before ever receiving a leadership position. However, there may be distrust between certain members on the team. Lack of trust among teammates can be just as disruptive and paralyzing as lack of trust in leaders.

Extreme Leaders realize trust within the team is the only way to reach the potential of the team and its members. Therefore, *Extreme*

Leaders proactively address the trust issue before it erodes team chemistry. Here are a few suggestions:

• *Address it through direct coaching* — The most direct way to address a trust issue with one or more members on the team is to confront the issue and coach them to a higher level of trust. Informed and involved leaders know when a teammate is not trustworthy, and they usually know the specific reasons for the distrust. While this can be a delicate coaching opportunity, Extreme Leaders find the courage to do it because they know people cannot improve if they don't acknowledge the problem. Once confronted and acknowledged, the problem can be solved through a joint plan of action.

• *Create team-building projects that rely on trust and teamwork* — Many times, the reason for lack of trust on a team is simply because the team members do not know each other well. Trust has to be earned, and this may take some time if teammates do not interact often. A good leader will create various projects or assignments that require groups of teammates to get to know each other better by working for a common result. Focusing on individual strengths for the benefit of a team assignment can build morale, improve skills, and foster greater trust among teammates.

• *Build rewards and recognition around the team* — Another way to reinforce team trust is to build some reward and recognition around *team results* versus *individual results*. If reward and recognition are predominantly structured for individual performance, the importance of teamwork and team chemistry is decreased. Instead, make sure to have some reward and recognition structured around team performance. This approach means everyone is dependent on each other to perform well. Teammates are more likely to help each other improve if some of their rewards and recognition are at stake.

• *Termination* — If trust has been severely weakened between an individual and the rest of the team, and it's not likely to be repaired, termination may be the best option. This step becomes necessary when the trust issue involves a serious violation of policy or is having a negative impact on the morale and performance of the team. An *Extreme Leader* knows that one or two people who are not trustworthy can destroy a team quickly. Don't be afraid to accelerate action in this instance. The sooner you remove the problem, the sooner you can find a quality replacement that could propel your team to new heights. (Note: Always follow your organization's process for appropriate termination.)

Measuring Trust

How do you measure trust between two or more people? How would you know if your trust bond as a leader is strengthening or weakening? What can you do about it?

It would seem that anything as important as trust would and should be measured. But how do you measure it? This is a valid question and one that could have a variety of answers.

In an indirect way, one might argue the performance results of a team are in direct proportion to the level of trust members have in their leader. Better performing teams tend to have higher trust bonds in their leaders and vice versa. Another approach can be as simple as asking each teammate to answer some direct questions about the level of trust in the leader, such as:

- Why do you trust me as a leader?
- What have I done to strengthen your trust in me?
- What areas could I improve in?
- What have I done to weaken your trust in me?
- What could I do differently that would increase your trust in me?

Leadership Trust Assessment

Building a leadership trust assessment tool could also be an effective way to measure trust between leaders and their teammates. This tool could be calibrated to produce a quantifiable metric as well as subjective feedback. It could also be used to establish a baseline result and then repeated at appropriate intervals to measure progress. Using some of the points made earlier under **Building Trust**, the following is an example of a leadership assessment tool that elicits feedback from each member of the leader's team:

Please rate the following statements 1 through 5 based on these ratings: 1 = strongly disagree; 2 = disagree; 3 = not sure; 4 = agree; 5 = strongly agree

Promises:
1. My manager keeps commitments. _____
2. My manager does what she says she's going to do. _____
3. My manager keeps promises to me. _____
4. My manager keeps promises to our team. _____
5. My manager does more than he commits to do. _____

Mistakes:
6. My manager freely and quickly admits mistakes. _____
7. My manager accepts full blame and responsibility for his/her mistakes. _____
8. When my manager makes a mistake, I trust him/her to make it right.. _____
9. My manager apologizes to individuals, when appropriate. _____
10. My manager apologizes to the team, when appropriate. _____

Actions:
11. My manager demonstrates a good work ethic. _____
12. My manager is reliable and dependable. _____
13. My manager is willing to perform any job on our team. _____
14. My manager's words are consistent with his/her actions. _____
15. My manager's actions motivate and inspire me. _____

Subjective Feedback:
- Why do you trust your manager as a leader?
- In what areas could your manager improve?
- What has your manager done to strengthen your trust factor?
- What has your manager done to weaken your trust factor?
- What could your manager do differently to increase your trust in him/her?

- Give one example of a promise or commitment your manager has made and kept (if applicable) or made and broken (if applicable).

Repairing Trust

Assuming leadership trust measures are in place and working well, the leader may discover a trust bond has been weakened or is deteriorating. When this situation occurs, what can a leader do to repair it? Repairing trust is not always easy but it can be done. The process will depend on the specific reasons for the distrust and the number of teammates affected.

For example, if a leader forgets to prepare and deliver a quarterly performance evaluation on a teammate, trust will likely slip *from that individual.* As soon as an apology is made and the evaluation delivered, repair begins. If the leader never forgets again or, better yet, does the evaluation early the next three quarters, trust will likely return to its previous level and may even strengthen. On the other hand, if a leader fails to get bonus recommendations in by the year-end deadline for the entire team, and no one receives a bonus, the leader may never be able to repair the damage. Trust may be destroyed, jeopardizing the leader's credibility and career.

It takes a sincere effort on the part of the leader to understand the reasons for a decline in trust, and it takes hard work to reverse the trend. Extreme Leaders are constantly working to behave in ways that build stronger trust bonds with their teammates. They protect and preserve their trust bond as if it were sacred. However, when faced with declining trust, *Extreme Leaders* will bravely face the situation head-on. They will quickly admit any mistake in judgement and apologize to all affected. They will then set out to repair the broken trust through actions and hard work. They realize they may have to prove themselves all over again to their teammates to re-earn their trust. While repairing trust is not easy, *Extreme Leaders* do whatever it takes to re-establish trust bonds.

Conclusion

"The future belongs to those who believe in their abilities."
— Abraham Lincoln

Extreme Trust *is* the magnet of *EXTREME Leadership*™; you cannot become a great leader without a strong bond of trust with your followers and teammates. At this very moment, the people around you have a certain perception of how much they trust you as a leader. What message have you been sending? Does this message attract or repel people?

As you continue to develop your leadership style, ask yourself these two questions: Do I have the courage to be an *Extreme Leader* and build Extreme Trust with the people around me? Will I inspire performance excellence by finding and using my personal courage to grow people and results? You will if you:

- Keep your promises
- Admit mistakes and are willing to apologize
- Develop an inspiring work ethic and walk your talk
- Confront and remedy trust issues within your team
- Find ways to measure trust by asking tough assessment questions
- Develop a strategy to continuously improve trust
- Work hard to repair broken trust

To paraphrase what Abraham Lincoln said above, the future belongs to leaders who believe in their abilities. As you create Extreme Trust with your teammates, they, too, will believe in your abilities, and you will become a wonderful example of Magnetic Leadership.

About Dave Timmons

*D*ave Timmons works with organizations to develop Extreme Leaders who inspire excellence and win in the marketplace. His passion is helping good managers find their courage to become great leaders. Dave's EXTREME Leadership™ programs help all levels of managers learn to lead with Heart (fearlessness), Mind (action) and Soul (emotions) in order to inspire others to performance excellence. Dave spent 25 years with two Fortune 100 banks, leading teams from 10 to 7500 employees to record sales and service performance. His EXTREME Leadership™ programs have inspired thousands of managers from coast to coast with clients such as Bank of America, Circuit City Stores, Honeywell International, AmSouth Bank, University of Central Florida, and Nielsen Media Research. Dave is co-author of Fantastic Customer Service Inside & Out and contributing author to Chicken Soup for the Soul® of AMERICA. Dave is proud to be a professional member of the National Speakers Association.

Contact Information:
Dave Timmons
Extreme Leadership Solutions
P.O. Box 340025
Tampa FL 33694-0025
Phone: (813) 792-9829
Fax: (813) 792-9810
E-mail: Dave@DaveTimmons.com
Website: www.DaveTimmons.com

Ten Strategies for Magnetic Leadership through your Positive Influence

by Susan B. Wilson, MBA, CSP

A young girl approached the balloon vendor. She gazed at the array of colors. The red was so pretty, the yellow shone like the sun, and the purple balloons reminded her of the huge grapes growing in Grandfather's garden. They were all so beautiful . . . but, in her eyes, none were as wonderful as the blue one. It was the color of the sky on a perfect summer's day. She reached into her pocket to pull out some money, but all she had were a few small coins, not nearly enough for the blue balloon she wanted.

Another child arrived and immediately gave the vendor the money for a balloon. He, too, liked the blue one and that is the one he chose. The girl watched him as he ran and played with it for a while, allowing it to bob up and down and all around. But before long, he lost interest in his balloon. A group of boys wanted to play, so he let go of the string and turned his attention to them. Wistfully, the little girl watched the blue balloon go up, up, and up until she could see it no longer.

She turned back to the vendor to ask, "Which balloon is your cheapest one?" The vendor, seeing beyond the question said, "This gray one is the cheapest. I can sell it for the money that you have in your pocket." The little girl thought a moment and then asked, "Will the gray balloon go as high in the sky as the blue one?"

"Oh yes," replied the vendor. "I know that it will. It's not what's on the outside that makes a balloon go up; it's what's on the inside."

And so it is with the way that we influence others through our leadership. "It's what's on the inside" that matters most for influencing others. Your internal resources of knowledge and skills, as well as your ability to trust and be trustworthy, are the most important factors in influencing those around you. We don't need to stand by wistfully and watch others rise up and up in their success. They may have a "blue balloon" style or message, but that is just one style! Like the array of balloons at the balloon vendor's side, there is an array of behaviors and actions that increase your influence for magnetic leadership.

Magnetic leadership is positive influence at work. Your positive influence attracts people and moves them into action to achieve desired goals. Your ability to increase your positive influence has no ceiling. You choose what you learn. You are the architect of the effective use of your skills. You have control over building consistent and constant trust in your relationships. No one strips you of your influence without your permission.

According to Warren G. Bennis, prolific author and teacher, "the most dangerous leadership myth is that leaders are born — that there is a genetic factor to leadership. This myth asserts that people simply either have certain charismatic qualities or not. That's nonsense; in fact, the opposite is true. Leaders are made rather than born."

Did you catch that? Leaders are made rather than born! With this wisdom in mind, let's consider ten specific strategies for increasing your influence to make you the magnetic leader that you are destined to become.

"All leadership is influence." — John Maxwell

1. Set specific, measurable goals and establish a plan to achieve them. Don't just think about your goals, set them — in writing. Make sure they are specific. Make sure they are measurable. *"Your mind, while blessed with permanent memory, is cursed with lousy recall. Written goals provide clarity. By documenting your dreams, you must think about the process of achieving them"* (Gary Ryan Blair).

Devise a plan to avoid the terrible three: Wander, Squander, and Ponder. The terrible three result in wasted effort and no action. With no goal to guide effort, we wander without focus, squander our resources, and ponder our next move. Blair's words remind us that clear goals with a plan focus precious resources of time, energy, and money.

An additional benefit to setting specific measurable goals and establishing a plan to achieve them is that we develop a proactive style often noticed by others. Relatively few people invest the time to identify what they want to achieve and how they intend to succeed.

Here's an example of this strategy at work. While facilitating a meeting, I overheard a conversation from two of the participants. Both were transportation superintendents for an aluminum company. One of them had pulled out a sheet of paper with her professional goals listed. She indicated that her boss wouldn't take the time to develop her goals with her, so she created them and asked for his approval of them. Her initiative had a positive influence on her colleague, who commented, "Wow, Alice. You really have yourself together. I'm going to try that with my boss."

Your goal setting and goal achievement are outward and visible signs of your effectiveness, which contributes to your influence.

2. Be right most of the time. *"There are things in your life you can control and there are variables you can't. The more diligent you are at controlling what you can, the more influence you'll have over your destiny. You have to figure out which are which"* — Carlton Young

Being right most of the time has to do with strengthening your skills of effective goal setting. But don't stop there. By continually strengthening your problem-solving, decision-making, priority-setting, and planning skills you increase the chances that you will be right most of the time. And if you're known for being right, people will listen to you.

While consulting at a power plant, I was interviewing a number of managers representing different levels of the organization. One of the questions was, "What manager do you most admire and why?" Without hesitation, a manager gave the name of a supervisor who reported to him. When asked why, he responded, "Because of her attention to setting goals, identifying problem areas, and strategies for resolving them. People just listen to this supervisor because she always seems to know what she is talking about."

Presenting data, facts, and rational argument in a constructive way builds influence and raises the probability that others will listen.

3. Use your power indirectly. *"You don't lead by hitting people over the head — that's assault, not leadership."* — Dwight D. Eisenhower

Few of us enjoy receiving orders or even being told what to do. Most of us desire the latitude to figure out things for ourselves. Here's a quick exercise to prove the point. Walk up to someone and ask him to hold up his left hand. Immediately, with the palm of your right hand, lean into and push into his palm. Most often, by far, the person immediately pushes back. Go ahead, push harder; it's not often he'll give in. He'll simply push back as well. What's the point? We don't like being pushed around physically or emotionally.

Greater influence over others' behavior results from *providing* guidelines for what is expected and *inviting* them to develop a plan. Give the specific goal, the time frame, and the resources available, but, when possible, encourage people to determine their own plan for achieving the desired result.

Encourage collaborative and/or consultative effort and avoid demands. Besides increasing your influence, you position others to develop theirs.

4. Choose talented employees. *"The function of leadership is to produce more leaders, not more followers"* — Ralph Nader

Hiring talent is a smart move that gets you noticed. Having the confidence to surround yourself with strong and competent people reflects well on your decision-making. Their skills and abilities help you achieve the results that lead to advancing your goals.

Whether at home, in the community, or at work, helping others develop and grow also benefits you. Frequently, one of the benefits that you receive from building others is their willingness to be an ally for you, even when they move on. Assist, develop, and help others achieve and you raise the probability that they will want to help you. For example, our business, Executive Strategies, Inc., employs one or two people at a time. We've been blessed with employees who have enormous talent, particularly in the area of their interpersonal skills. Over the past ten years, four people have worked with us. Each one, as she has made the decision to leave, has moved to a position even better suited for her gifts and talents. And each one, after having moved on, has made referrals to Executive Strategies that have enhanced our reputation and bottom line. Talented employees give as well as they get.

Recruit and hire great talent to develop even more positive influence.

5. Increase your knowledge and skills. You influence others by your willingness to continuously learn. John F. Kennedy claimed that, *"Leadership and learning are indispensable to each other."* Many of us agree. Others, looking to you for guidance, expect you to know what you are talking about. They expect you to inspire and instill confidence.

Develop a stance of "always becoming" rather than "always knowing." In doing so, you attract new information and experiences which contribute to your bank of knowledge and skills. Not long ago, I was at a seminar that a highly public figure also was attending. I noticed that he sat in the front row, pulled out a notebook of paper, and stayed busy throughout the session taking notes.

Yearn to learn and increase your influence.

"Leadership is the influencing of people to cooperate towards some goal which they come to find desirable." — Ordway Tead

6. Develop trust by talking from the same side of the table.
"Leadership has a harder job to do than just choose sides. It must bring sides together." — Jesse Jackson

Unfortunately, our communication and actions often create barriers in our relationships. Barriers that prevent us from liking one another as well as barriers that prevent us from taking the risk to be open and honest with one another often emerge. Our challenge is to minimize those barriers. Our opportunity is to establish a reputation for fair and honest relationships.

Consider this perspective on trust. Trust is that quality that communicates, "I like you; I'm willing to take the risk of trusting you. I'm likeable; you can take the risk of trusting me." Two key words are involved — like and risk.

The more trustworthy you are perceived to be, the less defensiveness you will see in others. A trustworthy stance establishes that you are trying to care as much about the other person's needs and goals as your own. Kelly Mooney and Laura Berheim, authors of *The Ten Demandments: Rules to Live by in the Age of the Demanding Customer* agree. The first "demandment" discussed in their book is, "Earn my trust." They say that you can forget about the other nine rules of influencing others if you don't master this one. My work over the years has transformed one of my opinions into one of my facts, "People will not give you their intellectual best if they do not first trust you."

A couple of years ago, I worked with the leadership of a coal mine. We were meeting for two days to initiate strategies for materially improving their safety record. I had been hired by the corporate office to travel to this Texas operation, and there was deep distrust and suspicion between the two sides of management and the union. After working with the nine men for a couple of hours that first day, the business agent for the union asked to meet with me privately. Tall, broad shouldered, dressed in jeans and spittin' tobacco into a Coca-Cola can, he drew himself up to his 6' 7" height (with boots!), looked way down at me, and drawled, "I don't know you, I don't like you, and I don't want you here." I looked directly back at him, allowed his words to settle between us and then asked, "Mark, is that all that you wanted to say to me?" "Yep," was his reply.

Never breaking eye contact, I said, "Okay, I've heard you. I understand you. Now let's go back in the room and see what we can accomplish." In that brief exchange, a seed of trust was planted with Mark. My response put me on the "same side of the table" with him. I listened, I accepted without defensiveness, and I positioned that we would work together. With both of us nurturing and feeding that "seed," our relationship and the relationships throughout the room improved miraculously over the two days.

Trust is essential for influencing others.

7. Believe in your position. *"The very essence of leadership is that you have a vision. It's got to be a vision you articulate clearly and*

forcefully on every occasion. You can't blow an uncertain trumpet"
—Theodore Hasburgh

Your certain trumpet is your conviction and *enthusiasm*. Facts and data are essential, but they mean even more when delivered with sincere enthusiasm. Your passion mobilizes attention. All other things being equal, the person who breathes enthusiasm is more influential. Your passion doesn't need to be noisy to be noticed. Remember Forrest Gump? Throughout the movie, his character achieved goal after goal after goal. As you watched, you could feel his certainty, his conviction for each accomplishment. In his simplicity, Forrest could articulate his goal clearly and with conviction. Forrest believed and in watching his belief, others believed.

When you believe, others watching your belief will believe.

8. Watch the clock. Carl Lewis, Olympic Champion, tells us, *"Life is about timing."*

We need to pay attention to the timing of our words and actions. Poor timing for making a request, giving a command, communicating a decision, or providing information can sabotage the best laid plan and hurt our positive influence. In fact, the best laid plans include a strategy for the timing of events and information.

Approaching your boss for additional resources just as she's leaving for a high pressure meeting with her boss is not good timing. Dealing with a conflict between two people during a meeting rather than waiting until there is privacy is poor timing. A company that releases coverage about salaries to their executives the same day that an article comes out about their union negotiations is not practicing good timing.

Support great thinking with great timing to enhance your influence.

9. Take others off the defensive. Author Dean Koontz adds to this view, *"Some people think only intellect counts: knowing how to solve problems, knowing how to get by, knowing how to identify an advantage and seize it. But the functions of intellect are insufficient without love, friendship, compassion and empathy."*

Keep communication open and flowing. Far too often, we use words and body language that set people up for frustration or even anger. Think about the "Junk Talk"^{sm} that so often is used. Junk Talk^{sm} is communication that diminishes trust and goodwill in relationships. Sarcasm, putdowns, unfair humor, yelling, swearing, making comparisons, and unfair criticism are all common forms of Junk Talk.^{sm}

On the other hand, WOW!^{sm} (Words of Wonder!) talk includes praise, affirmation, encouragement, and support that is specific and meaningful. WOW!^{sm} is language that builds bridges and positions people for effectively working together. WOW!^{sm} builds others up, Junk Talk^{sm} tears them down.

You don't have to accept the invitation to get angry from the Junk Talk^{sm} that so often erupts. Instead you can use WOW!^{sm} to welcome forgiveness, understanding, and encouragement. Junk Talk^{sm} invites others to think small; WOW!^{sm} encourages the very best from people.

Check your daily language to remove Junk Talk^{sm} and add WOW!^{sm} to your daily language to watch your positive influence soar.

10. Be a "care package." *"We control fifty percent of a relationship. We influence one hundred percent of it"* — Barbara Colorose

Consistently, our words and our actions are a package of care ... or not. And our care makes a difference to those we want to influence in a positive way. Who hasn't heard the saying, "No one cares how much you know until they know how much you care." But let's put a different spin on these words as we consider this tenth strategy.

"No one cares how much you know until they know how much you care *about yourself as well as others.*" Too often, we, in leadership positions, neglect our own needs in order to provide for others. This personal neglect often leads to diminished leadership effectiveness as our needs to receive become greater than our resources to give. Let's remember that as we accept and give care to ourselves, we enlarge our capacity to care for others.

Be a care package of thoughts, words, and actions. Share that care with yourself as well as others to influence your relationships in a healthy, positive way.

Our ideas for this chapter began with a reminder that it's what's on the inside that matters most for influencing others. Your internal resources of knowledge and skills, as well as your ability to trust and be trustworthy, are the most important factors for influencing those around you. Use these resources for effective action. Make a radical difference now. Give life to these ten strategies. Don't wait. Get started. Your opportunity is now. Begin.

> *"You don't have to be a 'person of influence' to be influential.*
> *In fact, the most influential people in my life*
> *are probably not even aware of the things they've taught me."*

— Scott Adams

About
Susan B. Wilson, M.B.A., CSP

*S*usan B. Wilson, M.B.A., CSP, is owner of Executive Strategies, Inc., a firm that works with organizations who are ready for greater value from their employees. As an expert facilitator and speaker, Susan leads employees to remarkable breakthrough performances. Her focused facilitation has helped end a coal mine fight and has earned her three NCAA Championship watches! Two of her highest profile programs are, "What's Draining Your Battery Pack?" and "Leadership with Class." Many of you use the products of Susan's clients: IBM, ALCOA, Maytag Appliances, Wells Fargo Banks and Albertson's Drug Stores, to name a few. She is a member of the National Speakers Association and has earned the prestigious Certified Speaking Professional (CSP) designation. Susan is a contributor to Chicken Soup for the Woman's Soul and she has authored two books and dozens of articles. She is also a popular resource for media.

Contact Information:
Susan Wilson
Executive Strategies, Inc.
1105 W. 12th Street South
Newton, IA 50208
Phone: (641) 791-7904
E-mail: susan@execstrategies.com
Website: www.execstrategies.com

FROM THE LEADER'S MESSAGE TO THE PUBLIC'S MEMORY

by Karen L. Anderson, M.A., Ed.S.

Most adults require five to 13 contacts before we are ready to buy a product or service. That's also true for buying ideas. If a leader wants to sell an idea, the leader must make several contacts. One may be as simple as mentioning the idea at the end of a staff meeting for people to think about — no decisions or actions are needed this early in the process. Another contact may be a conversation at the water cooler: "Have you thought any about that idea I suggested?" But this approach can become tedious unless we discover how to word and frame our messages into memorable images that can be retained and retrieved easily. Each retrieval can then become a contact that, sooner or later, will lead to action.

If the idea we are selling comes in an unclear message, we can expect frustrated followers and failed plans. Experts have three possible explanations for employees who fail to perform as a leader expects: employees are confused by what is expected of them, they lack commitment for the expectations, or they are opposed to the expectations. For instance, a supervisor directs an assistant to turn the lights on in each room of the business suite as the first task each morning. The assistant may not understand why this procedure is important because while growing up, the assistant was told to turn off lights when a room was empty. Consequently, the assistant begins Monday morning by making coffee, Tuesday morning with checking e-mail messages, and so on. Once the supervisor recognizes the delayed lighting, the leader can offer logical reasons for lighting all the rooms, such as its providing a security check for property stored in each room or a marketing technique that shows commuters on the street that this is a busy business office. The following morning, the assistant turns on all the lights first. If we want followers to comply, they must know why!

A leader inspires, encourages, and equips others to accomplish what they envision together. Magnetic leading requires three action verbs to ensure that the message compels action. These three M-words provide the structure for effective and memorable communication with your public: Move, Manage, and Mentor.

Move

Leaders must deliver the message in a package designed to assist memory. Only when a leader's public has impressions logged in memory will those images act as reminders to act. Using action verbs, concrete nouns, parallelism, rhyme, mnemonics, metaphors, stories, and numbers are some of the ways to package messages and move audiences.

What constitutes professional writing and speaking? Would you answer with a description of the word choices, considering the level of vocabulary and the tone of the message? Most people studying writing skills do. Which of the following sentences would you rather read in an e-mail: Sample A or Sample B?

Sample A: Previous to comprehending temporary memory characteristics, representatives of management frequently have the assumption that multisyllabic vocabulary selections are more demonstrative of professionalism than simplistic, memorable terminology is.

Sample B: Before understanding how short-term memory works, managers often assume complex words sound more professional than simple words do.

Most people prefer Sample B because it's shorter, simpler, clearer, and easier to understand than the first sample. In analysis, five characteristics surface: first, Sample A contains three abstract nouns instead of B's four concrete nouns and, second, three existence verbs to B's five action verbs. Consider using action verbs and concrete nouns as ways of tapping into the collective neurolinguistic style of your public, your audience. Suzette Haden Elgin, Ph.D., author of *Success with the Gentle Art of Verbal Self-Defense* (Prentice Hall, 1989), shows how these word choices can build rapport with readers and listeners. The field of neurolinguistic programming (NLP) continues to fascinate many leaders.

Also, Sample A's predicate is the tenth word, one position beyond the suggested depth for immediate understanding while B's predicate fell acceptably within the first nine words of the sentence. We understand sentences faster when the main verb enters early. Fourth, A contains three prepositional phrases to B's one. These clusters of words add conditions within the main idea of the sentence. Too many can confuse the audience.

Finally, Sample A exceeds the 22-word, short-term-memory limit while B's 18 words meet the memory guideline. The audience still remembers the beginning of sentence B by the time the end of the sentence arrives. Sample A hinders memory while B assists it. Perform a simple test by speaking any sentence aloud: if you can say it in one breath without gasping for air, your audience can remember it.

The author of *The Literate Executive: Learn How to Write Like a Leader* (McGraw-Hill, 2000), Laurie Rozakis, Ph.D., states that most executives take more than an hour to write a business letter at the cost of $75-100 per communication and major reports with a team of technical writers at the cost of $500,000 or more. Using the criteria for the analyses above could significantly reduce the typical costs. She writes, "According to a survey conducted by the International Business Communicators, communication yielded a 235 percent return on investment." Just think how that could be improved!

Leaders compose and followers remember B sentences. Word choices that create sensory impressions that we see, hear, touch, move, taste, and smell also create accessible messages that move people to thought and action.

The power of words is also demonstrated in Yale University's study of the twelve most persuasive words in America: you, guarantee, money, love, save, discovery, new, results, easy, health, free, proven. Roberta Roesch lists them in her book, *Smart Talk* (Anacom, 1989). A brief analysis of the words reveals their humanity and hope for happiness.

Leaders who use these words, mean them, and back them up with action as well as promise, share their humanity and hope for happiness through their messages and visions. These words get attention.

Another communication strategy, called parallelism, blends repeated form and function into balanced statements. An example is found in the famous parking lot scene in Fannie Flag's story, "Fried Green Tomatoes" (Universal Pictures, 1991), during which Kathy Bates's character, Evelyn, expresses her displeasure with the two women.

The driver steals the space Evelyn has patiently awaited.

Young Women: "Face it, lady, we're younger and faster."

(The women enter the grocery store. Evelyn rams their Volkswagen Beetle. They hear the commotion and return to the lot.)

Young Women: "Are you crazy?"

Evelyn: "Face it, girls, I'm older, and I have more insurance."

The leader uses rhythm and content to connect with the audience. Repetition of form appears in "Face it," the apostrophe in a contraction, the -er suffix, and "and."

The repetition of function brings "lady" and "girls" together, "young-" and "old-." Once our brains decode the first part of the pattern, the neurons are lined up, ready for the second part. Consequently, we comprehend and connect the images immediately.

During the O.J. Simpson trial, Attorney Johnny Cochran used another form of repetition: "If it doesn't fit, you must acquit!" The rhyme became a mantra, and the defendant went free. Rhythm, rhyme, and repetition were also favorite devices of Martin Luther King, Jr. Just consider his "I Have a Dream" speech. He was a master communicator who moved the U.S. into the Civil Rights Movement.

Mnemonic devices such as the three M-words help people remember concepts and steps in a leader's quest for success. Another example of a memory device follows; it is also a leader's tool.

Several years ago, a group of grandmothers who founded a non-profit nursery school and a group of young professional educators who wanted to obtain the school as a for-profit business disagreed regarding the way to transfer ownership. Both sides had hired attorneys. A liaison agreed to mediate. She used the FOCUS™ technique (frustrations, obstacles, consequences, utopia, and satisfaction). Locating a neutral territory for the groups to meet, the liaison asked 25 women to sit on the floor of her living room. In a wide circle, each could see all the others. The liaison passed index cards around and provided pens. She then asked all the women to individually record their frustrations concerning the transfer of the school's ownership. Silently, they wrote, "This is so stupid. Why can't this be simple?" Then they recorded the obstacles to a smooth transition as each experienced them. Names were probably noted: "Sally is power-tripping!" The current circumstance, if continued, would probably result in . . . "One-hundred-year-old-biddies who couldn't give up control of a fine cooperative school to the younger generation eventually died in a hump among the five-year-olds during naptime." Utopia represented the best-case scenario, such as "We won!" Finally, each woman wrote a statement describing what she could live with: "I want the school to survive and thrive for the benefit of the children of this community."

This process helped people reflect, starting with a specific gripe and ending with a realistic goal. Once the cards were written, each person read her final statement. The leader's job was now to keep both parties out of litigation by focusing on a common and noble goal: successful transfer of ownership for the sake of the children. The transfer was a success and the school continues almost twenty years later.

Leaders focus on the destination, allowing followers to travel on their own paths toward the outcome. Some will take detours, some will make extra pit stops, and others will race to the finish line. Perhaps there are occasions when a leader may have to tow some stakeholders who break down or get lost along the way, but most people will keep up and arrive safely. The effective leader keeps the big picture in focus, targets the destination, and knows how to offer encouraging remarks at the right time to keep everyone on track and on time. Being in the midst of committed leadership makes the travel an adventure.

Marlene Caroselli, Ph.D., notes how effective communicators

often use these literary devices, such as metaphor, in her book *The Language of Leadership* (Human Resource Development Press, 1990). The imagery based in the map metaphor is an example of how leaders enter the minds of their public.

Another technique leaders use to move their public is the story. Gerry Spense, Esq., wrote *How to Argue and Win Every Time* (St. Martin's Press, 1995) about the skill and spell of storytelling. It's a powerful way of inviting your public to experience an event or condition. This experience becomes convincing and has won over many juries to favor the lawyer's clients — based on the intent, if not the letter, of the law.

An example of a story comes from the president of Outdoor Construction, Inc., in the Greater Kansas City area. Lanson S. Hotchkiss learned about leadership from two family dogs, Echo and Griz, both Alaskan Malamutes. One day, coyotes ventured into the family's front yard while one-year-old Lanson played in the fenced back yard. Echo soared over the chain-links, chasing the pack of intruders. One coyote succumbed to Echo's speed and bared teeth. Echo firmly restrained the coyote by the throat until the others had crossed the yard's boundary. Then Echo released his victim, allowing it to scamper back to the pack. Echo then jumped the fence into the back yard to sit next to the child. Echo demonstrated strength and mercy. He was a protector.

Griz was Echo's son. Griz, twice as big as Echo, was known for throwing his weight around. A neighbor walking a dog might find Griz galloping toward them. Griz would go for the pet's underbelly. Griz's instinct and strength were untempered and unforgiving. He went for the kill even when there was little or no threat. Griz was a survivor.

Lanson loved both of his dogs, accepting their different personalities. Yet, he says, "I choose to be an Echo." Stories are powerful life histories.

Finally, numbers play a significant part in moving people to action. When we leave for the grocery store, having forgotten the list on the kitchen counter, we must weave the aisles of the store in search of the items on the list. Experience tells us we'll get some of the items, yet not all. Studies show that people remember best what is at the beginning and the end of lists and that most of us can comfortably remember only five to nine items. We all can easily remember three items: "the rule of three." So, the leader can use this information by giving followers three ideas, tasks, or reasons to remember at a time. Also, if a leader has 25 items that are important, the leader can categorize them into shorter lists of three to nine categories, with the most important information at the front and the back, to help the followers recall the message.

We are more likely to trust and act on what we understand immediately and remember instantly. A leader who uses a variety of techniques to project both an image and a message can move his or her public to achieve great potential.

Manage

Assess, decide, direct, resource, budget, assess again: managing has a lot to do with attitude and perspective, and so does fighting fires. The second M-word plays an integral part in interagency fire management, as the last few years have brought brutal wildland burns to several states.

Many of us grew up with Smokey the Bear's motto "Help Prevent Forest Fires." What we realize now is that fire's natural thinning effect allows fresh growth and new habitat for wildlife if the undergrowth and forest thickness are controlled a bit at a time. So says John Lissoway, U.S. Park Service veteran and fire management consultant, who interrupted his retirement to train firefighters at the national headquarters in Boise, Idaho. If no structures or human resources are at risk as a fire feeds itself upward along a mountain top, the fire may now be allowed to seek its demise in its own time. The fuel in the forests all over the nation has grown dense and unsafe. That's what happened in Bandelier National Monument, just outside Los Alamos in northern New Mexico's Jemez Mountains.

A "controlled burn" by park rangers had exploded in the shifting mountain breeze and soon surged toward the Los Alamos National Laboratory complex while incinerating almost 300 homes. James E. Rickman, former councilman in Los Alamos, New Mexico, fought his mother's insurance company for two years after her home disintegrated into skeletal iron and ashes in May of 2000. Jim lobbied in Washington,

D.C., for the Cerro Grande Fire Assistance Act to assist property owners in rebuilding their town and their lives. His tenacity won his mom the home she now shares with her cats and hummingbirds.

Another part of the fire story involves Lanson Hotchkiss's sister, Bree A. Hotchkiss, wildlife biologist and emergency medical technician, who served as a wildland firefighter with the Santa Fe National Forest in 2001 and as an engine-crew member in Eagle, Colorado, in 2002. She dares where few men and even fewer women will go or do. She fought the fire lines with saws and Polaskis (part shovel, part hatchet) for days on end with little food, sleep, or privacy. Nerves wear thin and tension thickens quickly during this hazard duty. Managing resources, mediating conflict, and sharing information become strategic events.

That's why briefings are essential; they protect wildland firefighters' lives. Having up-to-date operations and observations from field leaders who have pertinent experience in fighting fires benefits the entire crew. Answering questions is a large part of being an effective manager. Finding herself with more fire time than her supervisor, Bree took the initiative to question a decision to fight a fire when there was no immediate escape route available for the firefighters. The supervisor later thanked her for her diligence and rescinded his order.

A collaborative approach rather than a competitive and hierarchical one can stand a better chance of saving lives, especially when each team member is watching another's back, ready to put out the flames. Bree suggests that if you must confront someone, follow this trick: stand beside the person you are advising — shoulder to shoulder as a supportive position, not face-to-face, which is a competitive position. Bree says, "Be secure with who you are so you can listen to suggestions without thinking they're a threat to your authority. Comment on contributions by recognizing a good job when it's done." Bree is learning to manage like a leader: being assertive, showing initiative and gratitude, and being dependable.

Mentor

Mentors are enthusiastic, lifelong learners. Mentoring anchors the leader's message into memory by caring for others, delegating responsibilities, and developing future leaders.

Betsy L. Kay, Manager of Claims and Subrogation for the Williams Companies, Inc., in Tulsa, Oklahoma, believes that even in a worldwide oil corporation, leaders must care for individual employees, knowing their names and stories. She says that as a leader she wants her employees "to feel important to the corporation because the employees are the corporation." Empathy and compassion are required strengths for one who leads well.

Delegating is a form of mentoring, yet leaders struggle with it. Some think that it's easier or faster to do a job than to explain it to a subordinate or coworker. When we make decisions for the short term rather than the long run, we limit our own potential as well as that of others. We can perform better ourselves and help others do the same if we free ourselves from routine or simple tasks that we can train or encourage others to do. We can train our successors to take over when we move forward and upward.

Veterinarian Terry Wollen and fundraiser Judy Wollen devote their lives to training successors through Heifer Project International. They are currently stationed in Thailand where they educate donors and villagers in a simple economic opportunity. Their organization supplies cows, goats, and rabbits to families, and trains the adults in the care of the animals, which provide nourishment and economic possibilities. Children receive milk and food that keep them healthy and help them grow strong. Offspring of the animals then provide additional resources to other villagers who are trained by the original trainees. The economic and nutritional benefits are perpetuated, thus encouraging depressed populations to become self-sufficient.

Planning finds its way into religious organizations across the nation as well. Many hunger for strong leaders. The Roman Catholic Church is undergoing scrutiny for its policies in hiding wayward priests. But there is no hiding at the "Church with the Bridge." Steven J. Langhofer, senior pastor of St. Paul's United Methodist Church in Lenexa, Kansas, teaches "consensus leadership": he trusts his staff's judgments, gives them permission to dream and to initiate activity, and celebrates their accomplishments and experiments. He has witnessed too many church organizations that collapse when the lead person leaves. "An effective leader is going to replace himself or herself." He has evolved as a leader by moving from primarily a pastoral stance to a leader-development position. He actively and directly works with leaders and potential leaders, encouraging them to minister to the rest of the congregation. He speaks his message through their leadership.

Another mentor, Rudy Giuliani, former Mayor of New York City and current leadership consultant, was named *Time* magazine's "Mayor of the World." In his recent book, *Leadership* (Hyperion Press, 2002), and on Oprah Winfrey's television show, he cites three essential leadership principles:

1. Prepare relentlessly.
2. Study. Read. Learn independently.
3. Stand up to bullies.

His example of compassion, courage, perseverance, integrity, and justice comforted a nation in shock and a city in mourning. These are the principles and behaviors of a model mentor and a magnetic leader. Giuliani cared, delegated, and planned his succession in the aftermath of the September 11, 2001 tragedy.

It was that infamous date that made America a family. It was that tragedy that manifested a natural family system. Many studies show that when people become isolated, they become vulnerable to illness. Harvard Professor E.O. Wilson's current research in sociobiology indicates that being connected to a social and emotional system — such as a work team, congregation, or community — keeps us healthier and happier than being alone. What can we learn from this? Leaders know how to advise and advocate for each "family member" within any given organization and that process builds trust. People remember leaders who remember their people.

Once you master the three M-words — Move, Manage, and Mentor — you will exemplify Magnetic Leadership. Leaders understand that people need to hear, see, and experience a message multiple times. In the midst of a changing context, leaders must supply a sense of confidence, if not comfort, and a positive intent. They must model the message. Followers must trust the leader's message enough to integrate it into their lives and to make the necessary changes from the inside out — both within themselves and within an organization. Once people understand, commit to, and agree with the message, the action to create the vision follows.

About
Karen L. Anderson, M.A., Ed.S.

*K*aren L. Anderson, owner of Anderson Catalyst Training Services (ACTS), creates programs that target persuasive communication strategies. She helps her clients plan and take action. Karen personalizes services for individuals and customizes presentations for organizations that want to improve current performance and relationships. She has won multiple awards for her teaching, speaking, and writing and has delivered presentations from coast to coast. She holds degrees and postgraduate work in adult education and instructional development, communication skills, business management, and behavioral sciences. Karen believes the quality of life hinges on our choices in daily decisions and the connections we choose with others. Her motto is: "Our ACTS-ion Says It All!" A member of the National Speakers Association and the American Society for Training and Development, Karen has developed and delivered curriculum for several universities. Her experiences as a certified trainer and developer, an adjunct professor, a writing coach/editor, a business consultant, and a state-approved mediator, all add real-life insights and laughs for her audiences. Her best-selling topics include "Professional Writing and Proofreading," "Train-the-Trainer," "Super Supervisory Skills," "Meeting and Minutes Management," "Collaborative Confrontation and Dispute Resolution," and "Customer Server: You ARE the Organization." Clients include telecommunications companies, federal and military agencies, city governments, corporations, and non-profit organizations.

Contact Information:
Karen L. Anderson
Anderson Catalyst Training Services (ACTS)
7923 Noland Road
Lenexa, KS 66215-2528
Phone: (913) 492-3881
Fax: (913) 492-5054
E-mail: karen @acts-ion.com
Website: www.acts-ion.com

The 3 C's of Life and Leadership

by Candy Whirley

For most people the 3 C's remain the biggest obstacles to success in both their professional and personal lives. These obstacles become the keys to successful leadership for those who invest the time to understand and master them. The 3 C's are creativity, communication, and change. All three will be covered in this chapter. I will also share activities I've used in my workshops to help participants truly understand the importance of each quality.

The reason my title is "The 3 C's of Life and Leadership" is that you have to have these qualities at home, too. I have heard participants say, "I'm going to start using these strategies at home with my children" or "this will work with my spouse."

Enjoy this chapter, and, as you're reading, think about how these concepts will work in your professional as well as your personal lives.

"I wanted to create a company where people dare to try new things — where people feel assured in knowing that only the limits of their creativity and drive, their own standards of personal excellence, will be the ceiling on how far and how fast they move."
— Jack Welch

Creativity is a gift we have had since childhood . . . find it.

Once when I was a kid, my neighborhood friends and I were bored, and we wanted to play something the whole group could play. We had access to a big field by an old house. We had a bat, no baseball, but a rubber kickball. Did that stop us? No. This was the best baseball game we ever played! When we hit that rubber ball it soared, and we could throw the ball at the base runner to make an out. You can't do that with a baseball! Little did we know how creative we were being. That's not all, we went one step further. We believed that three bases were too boring, so we made six bases, plus home! We played until dark.

What do children do about obstacles? They create, they invent, they change, and they play. Stop and think for a moment about your childhood and how creative you were with those obstacles. One study showed that about two percent of all adults are creative, 10 percent of seven-year-olds are creative and 90 percent of all five-year-olds are creative. What does this say? As adults we tend to push back our creativity and our childhood playfulness. You can get it back and take advantage of it in your organization. Use your obstacles to your benefit to be a more creative leader.

The best way that you can get those creative juices flowing is by laughter. When is the last time you laughed at work? I mean a deep-down belly laugh, either at yourself or with others. Researchers have found that children under the age of seven years old laugh on the average 100 times a day. Adults laugh 3-4 times a day. According to a study by the University of Minnesota, the top children in intelligence and social skills from grades 4-8 had the best sense of humor. How do you get that sense of humor and laughter back? In my Creativity Day Camp for Leaders, I use a technique I call the ABC Game to help cultivate an environment of humor and laughter and to initiate creative and innovative ideas. I use it in brainstorming sessions.

I start the session out with an icebreaker to teach participants the rules of the game. First, they are asked to get in a giant circle. When you ask them to do this, the laughter and the child start emerging. Think about it: what game did we play when we were young and had to get in a circle? You got it: Ring-Around-The-Rosie! Some of your team members will even try to hold hands, which again will cause laughter. The creativity has already begun. I've done this game with groups as small as 8 and as big as 80. Second, I tell the group that we are all going to tell a story, but this is not your average story; this story will be told in alphabetical order. Third, I ask the group for a subject. I tell them it can be outrageous! I've had participants throw out subjects such as the zoo, menopause, or pickles. Tell your group again it doesn't matter what the subject is; just let them shout the subjects out and you pick one. Fourth, I explain that there are only two rules, and if someone breaks a rule, I have them try again.

Rule 1:

Each member has to start with a successive letter of the alphabet. The idea can be a sentence or one word, but it has to start with the letter that the group is on. (Example below)

Rule 2:

Let the group know that the game needs to go quickly. You don't want them to ponder too long about their ideas. (The less time they have the more outrageous the story gets, and the more laughter, the more creative they will be! Remember the first time is for fun, just to loosen them up.) As the facilitator I always start the story.

For example, the subject is the zoo:

First person in the circle, (usually the facilitator): **A** long time ago I went to the zoo . . .

Next person: **B**engal tigers are my favorite . . .

Next person: **C**ats are the best part of the zoo . . .

Next person: **D**on't you think the zoo smells? . . .

Next person: **E**eeeks! . . .

Next person: **F**un is what I have at the zoo . . . Etc.

The game goes through the entire alphabet. If the group is small, keep going around until the entire alphabet has been used. If the group has more than 26 members, start over with A. Sometimes the subject changes during the game. I let my participants know that it's O.K. if the subject changes, and I encourage them to be outrageous, and to think outside the box. They do! Now your group knows how to play the ABC Game. What does this have to do with creativity? When you are ready for your brainstorming session, whether it's new policy ideas, mission statement ideas, or simply solutions to problems, your team will be ready. This game loosens up the group and promotes innovation and creativity and lets them know it's all right to be outrageous.

In one of my leadership sessions, I ask my participants to brainstorm about how to overcome mistakes leaders make in their organizations, such as "lack of communication in the workplace" or "doesn't create a positive work climate." I break the participants into small groups of 5-10, assign one group the letters A-M and the next group N-Z. If you have more than two groups, just repeat the letter assignments. I sit back and watch many different ideas come from each group. The ABC Game stretches their brains to new, more creative ideas beyond their belief. Here are some ideas that have come from the ABC Game from across the country:

Brainstorming subject, lack of communication in the workplace:

Always let the staff know of any changes.

Be sure communication is timely.

Catch someone doing something good and tell them.

Days without communication are days of missed ideas.

E-mail will work in some cases.

Friendly environment.

Give someone a thank you note.

Have an open door policy.

I is not a letter in TEAM!

Just do it!

Knowledge.

Laughter.

Make your team aware of changes with a state of the organization meeting.

When I first started using this strategy for brainstorming, I noticed the ideas were more creative, and the participants loved it. I also got more ideas from the group than I did before.

I gave you the A-M example, take two minutes and generate the N-Z ideas of how to overcome lack of communication in the workplace and see how creative YOU truly are . . . GO!

N	U
O	V
P	W
Q	X
R	Y
S	Z
T	

Amazing isn't it?

Remember creativity is a gift we've had since childhood . . . find it, and watch your teams and your organization soar.

"Creativity and play need each other. A person might be able to play without being creative, but he sure can't be creative without playing!"
— Kurt Hanks & Jay Parry

Communication is essential for human interaction and understanding . . . use it.

It's hard in our busy world to pay attention to our communication skills, yet it's a must if we want to be an effective leader. According to Albert Mehrabian, 7 percent of our communication is vocabulary, 38 percent is pitch and tone, and 55 percent is nonverbal.

Verbal communication is more than knowing what the words mean. It's the art of choosing your words wisely for any situation. I've learned that one of the most difficult situations leaders encounter is giving constructive feedback in a straightforward yet positive way. Although difficult, constructive, straightforward feedback is essential if positive relationships are to be maintained. I teach a method that I call the Like Best and Next Time technique, LB's and NT's for short. This is language I learned when I attended a workshop on how to become a better presenter. With practice using this language, you will enhance your verbal communication skills and your working relationships. Let me give you an example of how the Like Best and Next Time technique was used with me at the workshop I attended.

I had to do a 15-minute presentation on Leadership Skills. I did this presentation in front of my supervisors and peers. While I was doing the presentation, the group was evaluating me by observing and taking notes.

When I was finished, they verbally gave me constructive feedback, after looking at their notes, by using the Like Best and Next Time language.

The group's feedback:

"Candy, I really *liked* your humor in the introduction and how you interacted with the audience. *Next time* I would slow down a little. The presentation was supposed to be 15 minutes and it was 12 minutes. Before you sit down Candy, I want to add that I really *liked* your activity that was relevant to the lesson you were teaching the group."

The Like Best and Next Time language is this simple. It's up to you as a leader to be proactive and think ahead of time about what you're going to say to your employee. Some key points to consider before you try this new language.

- Always start with what you like best about your employee. This approach builds confidence and receptivity to the constructive feedback.
- If you go back to the example, you will notice the words "but" or "however" were not used before they gave me my constructive feedback (next times). What happens when someone gives you a positive or "like best," then gives you a "but" or "however?" You guessed it. It negates all of the positive things they just said. Participants in my workshops have asked me why they shouldn't use "however," and I tell them that "however" is just a soft "but"!
- You end with a positive, something else you like best about the employee. You want your employee leaving the conversation with self-esteem intact. Jack Welch, former CEO of GE wrote in his book, *Jack Straight from the Gut*, "When people make mistakes, the last thing they need is discipline. It's time for encouragement and confidence building. The job at this point is to restore self-confidence."

This technique is a sandwich approach. We are sandwiching the "next times" between the "like bests." To get the best results you must practice, practice, practice. Get your colleague, spouse, or friend to let you role play. That's what I do in my workshops. It works; the hard part is not to say "but" or "however." If you have trouble ending with a like best statement, write down all of the positive things about the employee ahead of time so you are ready. You can do this by looking at your employee's past evaluations or positive notes in their personnel files. The Like Best and Next Time technique will be one of the most effective communication techniques you use, yet, it will be up to you to practice and use the language. I promise it will enhance your working relationships with your employees as well as your personal relationships.

> *"The higher you go, the wider spreads the network of communication that will make or break you. It extends not only to more people below, but to new levels above. And it extends all around, to endless other departments and interests interacting with yours."*
> — Donald Walton

We also have to be aware of HOW we say these words. Our pitch and tone can make or break what we are trying to express. How many times do we create misunderstandings over the way we've said something? For example, have you ever been in a conversation with a colleague, employee, or significant other and you said, "I don't understand why you are upset; this is what I said." And the other person will respond, "Well, it's the way you said it!" That is pitch and tone, the way we say things. Whether it is professionally or personally, we have to be aware of how we say things. Let me give you a mini exercise. (I hope you are reading this privately because I need for you to do this out loud to get the point.) Say "Oh" out loud. Now say "Oh" like you're mad, say "Oh" like you're glad, say "Oh" like you fell in the mud, say "Oh" like you're in love! Now after you finish laughing at yourself, think about the many meanings "Oh" can have by simply changing your pitch and tone. Do these exercises at your next team meeting to have the whole team get a chuckle and at the same time realize we have to be aware of how we express ourselves in every situation. With this new awareness, you and your team can alleviate communication disasters and enjoy more successes.

Body language calls for awareness as well. Leaders have to constantly and consistently be aware of what their body language could be saying because it is 55 percent of our communication. Your nonverbal language can redefine your message with a simple gesture. Has an employee ever come up to you with a personal problem when you are busy or deep in thought? You might nicely say, "Can I help you," yet your body language might indicate, "I don't care," because your eyes have slightly rolled or worse yet, you are not making eye contact at all. Without being aware, you have your arms crossed across your chest. What does this say? It may say, "You are not important," or "I don't have time for you," or "My work is more important than your problem."

We all at some time in our busy lives give these nonverbal signals at home and at work. The key is to be aware before relationships are damaged. Whether you are the CEO, supervisor, or team leader of an organization 85 percent of your professional success is based on relationships; only 15 percent is based on your technical skills. Cherish your working relationships.

Change is a must in today's society . . . roll with it.

I am writing this portion of the chapter as we near the first anniversary of 9/11. This event changed our world and the way we think about the people in our lives. That's what I want to focus on in this portion of the chapter, changing our attitudes about the people that we work and live with. One of the most common things I hear in my workshops is, "It's not the job stressing me out, it's the people." People are different in many ways, but as leaders we need to embrace those differences, change our attitude, and learn to work with all personalities.

"Can you imagine a whole hockey team of goalies?
Or a football team of quarterbacks? It doesn't make sense.
In the same way, organizations require diverse talents to succeed,
each player taking his part."

— John Maxwell

Personality differences have always been a source of conflict. It's a subject that I have grown passionate about. If you ever have a chance to take a personality profile test, do it. It will not only give you insight and understanding of yourself and others, it will reveal to you how these differences are actually strengths that can be harvested for the benefit of all. There are a variety of personality profile tests to choose from, such as Meyers Briggs, DISC and Self Profile. In my seminars I use an approach that recognizes four different personalities, which I have briefly outlined below. Each outline includes a phrase describing the personality, several characteristics of the personality, and a type of bird to help in identifying with the personality.

The "get appreciated" personality.
Characteristics:
- Risk takers
- Thrive on change
- Very direct
- People-oriented
- Likes recognition
- Dislikes indecision or waiting
- Bird: a peacock. The peacock has to get attention by showing off its brilliant feathers.

The "get it done" personality.
Characteristics:
- Organized
- Goal-oriented
- Determined
- Task-oriented
- Likes loyalty
- Dislikes when people don't get to the point
- Bird: a hawk. The hawk has its eye on everything as it soars.

The "get along" personality.
Characteristics:
- Patient
- Good listener
- Devoted
- People-oriented
- Likes affirmations

- Dislikes insincerity
- Bird: a dove. The dove values peace and loves everyone.

The "get it right" personality.
Characteristics:
- Attention to detail
- Meticulous
- Fact finder
- Task-oriented
- Likes perfection
- Dislikes over-assertiveness
- Bird: an owl. The wise owl has to know everything.

Looking at all of these personalities and their characteristics, do you see yourself? Do you see the people that you work with or the people you live with? Do you see why some people drive you crazy! We are not alike, so we must find ways to adapt and have better relationships.

For example, when you are working with a peacock you need to give him or her flexibility. Remember, peacocks like change. This would be a great person to cross-train or put in charge of a committee working on a short-term project. We have to be open to the peacock's creativity. Most importantly, give peacocks credit for their hard work and great ideas.

The hawk needs to be in control of its own destiny. Hawks like to know what's going on in the organization. Keep them in the loop. This person makes a good leader. They're usually our CEO's and directors of our organizations. They are the best people to bring structure back to an organization going through change.

The dove is the peacemaker. Doves are very team-oriented people. They are great gatekeepers at team meetings. The doves make sure every person's opinion is heard. This person is not a loner, so make sure the dove is given opportunities to interact with others.

The owl has great ideas; give her time, ask her opinion, and you will get results. This person is an expert at gathering facts and data; acknowledge his expertise. Under pressure this person is calm and steady. You will not find a more dependable person.

As leaders we need to recognize, embrace, and adapt to different personalities. We need to change our attitude about the folks that we work with and live with. We need to change our focus from, "They are not like me" to, "What is their expertise" and use that strength to improve our organizations as well as our relationships.

By practicing the skills above, you will be well on your way to mastering the 3C's of Life and Leadership, and you will become an effective leader with influence, in both your professional and personal lives.

"An eagle environment is one where the leader casts a vision, offers incentives, encourages creativity, allows risks, and provides accountability. Do that long enough with enough people, and you'll develop a leadership culture where eagles begin to flock."
— John Maxwell

References

The 21 Irrefutable Laws of Leadership. John C. Maxwell. Nashville Tennessee: Thomas Nelson Publishers, 1998.

Jack, Straight From The Gut. Jack Welch and John A. Byrne. New York, New York: Warner Books, Inc., 2001.

Self Profile. A Division of Rockhurst University Continuing Education Center, Inc. Overland Park, Kansas: National Press Publications, 1987.

Wake Up Your Creative Genius. Kurt Hanks and Jay Perry. Menlo Park, California: Crisp Publications, Inc., 1991.

World Wide Web, *Quotes to Inspire you.* http://www.cybernation.com/victory/quotations/authors/quotes walton_donald.html

Working Women's Communication Survival Guide. Ruth Herman Siress. Englewood Cliffs, New Jersey: Prentice Hall, 1994.

About Candy Whirley

Candy Whirley is president of SBG Services, a training and consulting company that helps organizations develop skills in leadership, team building, creativity, communication, and relationship building. She holds a B.S. in Speech Communications with an emphasis in Human Relations, which has proved to enhance her workshops and conferences. Candy's broad professional background includes experience in entertainment, restaurant, non-profit, religious and community services. As president of SBG Services, Candy's main goal is what she calls edu-tainment: learning while having fun. Her training topics include leadership skills, stress management, and team building. Additionally, she speaks at women's conferences and hosts Creativity Day Camps. She has delivered training to management and staff for organizations such as: General Motors, Federal Aviation Administration, Hallmark Cards, Sprint, Kauai Chamber of Commerce, and various education administrations. Candy holds active memberships in the National Speakers Association and the American Business Women's Association.

Contact Information:
Candy Whirley
SBG Services, LLC
4409 NE 48th Terrace
Kansas City, MO 64119
Phone: (816) 455-4753
Fax: (816) 455-4753
E-mail: cwhirley@kc.rr.com

Facilitative Leadership: Honoring the Minds and Hearts of Others

by Linda Logan-Condon

"The very essence of all power to influence lies in getting the other person to participate."

— Harry A. Overstreet

Today, our organizations, our institutions, and our communities are crying out for great leadership. Clearly, we are in a time and place in our history where we have not been before. Truly effective leadership requires we take what we have learned from the past and continue to explore the very essence of leadership and how it applies to our collective future.

As a business owner, consultant, and coach, one of the most challenging and rewarding aspects of working with great leaders is their willingness and ability to create and sustain a culture of high participation and involvement. Exceptional leaders know how to bring out a high degree of excellence in those around them. They believe the answers we are searching for lie within the people around them . . . not just within themselves. And, finally, they emphasize the importance of balance between content and process. Task results and interpersonal relationships are equally important in the success of any organization. As we continue to move through the age of information and technology into the relationship age, we must not forget the importance of people, participation, and partnership.

In this chapter, you will gain an appreciation for "out of the box" leadership. Leaders are not just those individuals who reside in the box on the organizational chart. Leadership is everyone's business, and developing a facilitative mindset is essential for leading from any position. While many understand the philosophy of leadership, when it comes to the practical aspects of what an effective leader *actually does*, the picture is less clear.

In addition, this chapter will focus on the practical aspects of being a facilitative leader. In essence, I will share with you a number of tools, tips, and processes for improving your ability to facilitate within the context of leadership.

Value-Added Behaviors

So, what exactly does a facilitative leader do? The facilitative leader first and foremost *inspires* and *empowers* the work group or team to be productive. In addition, he or she maintains a balance of attention on both the technical-business issues and the interpersonal interactions that surround the issues. A facilitative leader realizes the benefits of balance. If all a leader does is focus on technical-business issues, eventually the interpersonal issues will require attention. On the other hand, if leaders focus only on the interpersonal issues, the work may not get done. Our organizations need both.

Ultimately, the facilitative leader establishes a climate which supports people to do the following:

1. To fully contribute their ideas.
2. To voice fears, concerns, wants, and needs.
3. To be creative and innovative when addressing issues.
4. To collaborate when solving problems.
5. To resolve conflicts constructively.
6. To participate in the decision-making process.
7. To achieve consensus on implementation strategies.
8. To buy in and commit when implementing action plans.
9. To own their successes and failures.
10. To create and adhere to a set of operating procedures, norms,

and ground rules.

Traditionally, leaders lead from a mindset of someone who is supposed to have all the answers, make all the decisions, provide the vision, mission, and values for the organization while maintaining full control and responsibility for resources, budget, and outcomes. Given the chaos surrounding our organizations today, successful leadership requires new and different skills. Successful leaders today come from a different mindset than the past. New leadership believes others in addition to themselves have the answers, share in decision-making, provide input into vision, mission, and values, and share both control and responsibility for the outcomes. To lead from any position requires the skills of a great facilitator.

The Ask — Tell Difference

In my work with clients, I am often asked to differentiate between the behaviors demonstrated by a "Meeting Manager" vs a "Facilitative Leader." Below is a list of "Meeting Manager" and "Facilitative Leader" behaviors. Read through the list and see if you can determine the difference for yourself.

Meeting Manager Behaviors

- Kicks off the meeting.
- Leads participants in discussion.
- Explains the meeting purpose, goals, and priorities.
- Creates a "climate" for the meeting.
- Calls for input and information.
- Examines consequences of proposed and actual decisions.
- "Manages" disruptive behavior.
- Takes action to resolve impasses.
- Checks the amount of agreement on a particular issue before moving to closure.
- Suggests a compromise when consensus cannot be reached.
- Maintains control, power, and responsibility for decisions.
- Adjourns the meeting.

Typical Facilitative Leadership Behaviors

- Asks how clear the purpose, goal, or issue is.
- Has participants reframe an issue into a goal statement.
- Ensures all participants have a chance to speak on each issue.
- Asks how widely shared a particular concern or feeling is among participants.
- Goes around the room to check options and opinions.
- Encourages participants to respond to one another's ideas and opinions in terms of agreement, disagreement, or indecision.
- Ensures participants voice concerns, fears, wants, and needs.
- Praises everyone's efforts and ideas.
- Guides participants through a consensus decision-making process.
- Shares observations about how well the participants are or are not working together.
- Points out when participant's ideas are being attacked.
- Comments on conflict and asks how the conflict might be resolved.
- Points out disruptive behaviors which create defensiveness and impede progress.
- Provides suggestions on alternate behaviors that would lead to a more productive discussion.
- Makes suggestions on how to resolve impasses.

While the role differences may appear minor to some, the impact on the team or work group is significant. The bottom line is, "People support what they create." Clearly, the behaviors of the facilitative leader encourage participation and involvement, focus on both task and relationship, and put control into the hands of the participants. If we want people in our organizations to be self-responsible, we must be inclusive.

Increasing Ownership

There are a variety of roles one can play when guiding a team to high performance. Each role is manifested by the amount of control and direction exhibited by the leader. The roles range from low to high control and direction beginning with the role of "Pure Facilitator"; "Facilitative Leader," "Formal Leader," and "Manager."

In addition, ownership for problems, solutions, innovations, failures, and successes also proceeds along a range. Ownership is determined by the amount of control and direction exhibited by the team versus the formal leader. The more control and direction a formal leader or manager exhibits, the more only he or she owns the issues and the outcomes.

The more one stays in the facilitative leader role, the more the team will own its issues and take responsibility for ensuring its success. A team moves more slowly in the beginning with a facilitator leader; however, the team will be more likely to reach high performance. Most organizations will not tolerate a pure facilitative role. Moving into the facilitative leader role is the ideal alternative.

Getting People to Participate

Once you have made the decision to move into the role of the facilitative leader, actually making it happen can be a bit of a challenge. Finding ways to focus and redirect those who talk too much is one thing, getting people to participate is another. Over the years I have found "drawing out the silent" requires a great deal of skill and focus. Below I have listed forty-five tried and true facilitation strategies that work.

1. To prevent restriction of opinions and suggestions by participants out of deference to the formal leader's point of view, have someone else lead off the discussion. Hold off on the formal leader presenting his/her viewpoint until much later after numerous alternatives have been offered. The formal leader's strongest move is often to support a point voiced by someone else.

2. When a group is composed of a mix of status levels, try working up the pecking order instead of down to encourage a wider spread of views and ideas. Be sure to ask the "junior" members for contributions only within their experience and competence.

3. Draw out the silent. Probe those who are silent out of inhibition or indifference, always being sure to express interest in their

ideas . . . even if the majority does not express agreement. Be equally attuned to silence which may reflect hostility. Concerns are better out than in. If concerns are not voiced, follow-through on commitments will never happen. Try these techniques for dealing with the "clam":

- Call on him for his experience or specialty.
- Alert her in advance that a certain topic is going to come up. Ask her to prepare a comment. When the moment is right, feed a pre-agreed cue line.
- Don't put her on the spot. Pose questions that allow room to maneuver, such as, "Did you ever run into this kind of situation when you were in the field?"
- Give him time to compose what he is going to say. Call on one or two others first, thus tipping him off and giving him a chance to prepare himself. Be careful not to cut off or put down other participants to protect the clam or to wrench the converstion around to set things up for him.

4. Acknowledge members, specifically the quiet ones, after every contribution by a positive nod or smile in their direction. Acknowledgement does not have to be verbal. Putting their idea on a flipchart or whiteboard emphasizes they have been heard and their contribution is important.

5. When identifying causes or potential solutions to a problem, use the "nominal group" technique. Give members two minutes of quiet time to write down as many ideas as they can think of. Then call on each employee to share one idea. Start with the quiet ones first so their ideas won't be presented by the talkers. Go around the room a second time asking for another single item. Scribe all ideas regardless of their feasibility — don't edit or you will kill all future participation.

Forty Five Facilitation Tips

1. Start on time! End on time!
2. Make your opening comments short! Get the team involved

within 2-3 minutes after your first statement. A team sitting passively in the first 5-8 minutes of a meeting conjures up a "typical meeting."
3. Have a "Suggested Agenda" written on the flipchart before the meeting begins. Have the team review the agenda, revise topics and outcomes where needed, decide on the order of topics, and the time periods for each topic.
4. Checkmark each agenda item as it is completed during the course of the meeting.
5. To kick off the ground rules discussion, ask: "If this was a great meeting in which everyone felt comfortable and could readily contribute, what would be happening?"
6. Have the team define terms used in ground rules: "confidentiality," "consensus," "leave rank outside the door," "everything stays in the room that's said," etc. There are very different operational definitions of these words among team members! Clarify, so failed expectations are minimized.
7. Don't have people raise their hands in order to get a chance to speak. This rule generally makes them feel like grade school kids. If this is a formal ground rule the team has agreed to, then accept it.
8. Write down the "heart" of every participant idea and every participant question. Don't wait for consensus to build among members before writing down something. Don't wait for a "worthwhile" idea before writing it down. You do not evaluate as a facilitator leader — you write! Detailed flipcharts give the team a sense of momentum, highlight disagreement more readily, and show the team when they are rambling or repeating themselves.
9. When you comment on the quality of one person's comment, you must do the same for all others. It is easier to make no evaluative statements!
10. Make the process of taping flipchart sheets on the wall as quick and simple as possible. On occasion, practice active listening as you're walking from the wall back to the flipchart to signal to

the team you're tracking right along with them.
11. If you can do so smoothly and quickly, alternate between two colors for each idea you write on the flipchart. People can find and read comments on sheets much faster when alternating colors are used.
12. Don't cross any written item off the flipchart unless you look at everyone in the group and get buy-in from everyone including the author of the item. Make eye contact! Don't blindly follow the preferences of a vocal minority.
13. If someone says, "You didn't put my idea up there," apologize immediately and write it on the flipchart.
14. Instead of using the title "Parking Lot" for tangential concerns, title the sheet "Concerns We Need to Address." "Parking Lot" can convey park and forget it.
15. During a break, number and title all flipchart pages if you have not done so during the discussion.
16. Insist members stick to the current topic.
17. Note ground rules and enforce them.
18. Enforce time limits. Occasionally note time remaining on agenda item. Note the amount of time behind schedule, if any. Ask the team if they want more time for a current agenda item discussion, how much more time, and which subsequent agenda items they will reduce the discussion time on.
19. If you're in facilitative leader role and you are a member of the team, you can use the word "we" most of the time. If you're in facilitative leader role and you are not a member of the team, use the word "you" most of the time. The choice of pronoun indicates who is responsible for meeting results.
20. Be aware of your "air time." Intervening and talking too frequently signals your nervousness as a facilitative leader. It is also a subtle way of controlling the team when you are uncomfortable with a team's process and outcomes. Too little talking when disruptive behavior is occurring is abdication on your part. How-

ever, if you must err, err on the side of not facilitating enough.
21. Almost any question asked of the facilitative leader should not be answered. Just say: "Good question for the team to address. What do you think?" Remember "empowerment" means letting people find their own answers. If you are a member of the team and have data no one else has, then it is appropriate to answer the question.
22. The facilitative leader can share a few of his/her strengths/experience in a get-acquainted exercise to model what you want from the team. Do not write your strengths or experience on the flipchart unless you are an actual member of the team.
23. Be sure to wrap up any get-acquainted activity by relating it to the task at hand. Ask:
    - "Which of these talents will be especially important to the project?"
    - "When you look at your list of talents and skills, who has a skill you would like to learn?"
    - "How might your diverse talents get you in conflict with one another?"
    - "Where are there skill gaps that the group will have to compensate for?"
24. Facilitating a group through the customer identification process:
    - Not really knowing who the customers are is typical in a team.
    - Not even knowing the chain of command is common.
    - Drawing an organization chart identifies gaps in people who are customers that the team forgot; how weak the links are between team members and the customers; and whether the project has a powerful enough sponsor.
    - Questions to get a team started on customer identification: "How did this team form?" "Who got you together?" "Who is going to evaluate your work when you're done?" "What do you understand to be your goal?" "Who is the most interested in this goal?" "Who might squash or block your efforts to

accomplish the goal?" "Who might push your efforts and recommendations through?"

25. When team members brainstorm, remind them of the rules: no interruptions, no evaluation of ideas, focus on quantity and not quality.
26. When brainstorming, keep reminding the team, "Let's list options first and evaluate later."
27. Don't fall into the trap of giving all of your attention to those who participate actively.
28. When there is a great deal of urgency to move to task, you may need to move into being more assertive as a facilitative leader. Bring a clear-cut structure to the team to get the members on track and focused on accomplishment.
29. Remember to let go of your agenda timetable when "people" issues surface in the group. The more you smooth over conflict in order to stay on task the more likely your efforts will fail.
30. Be prepared to serenely accept the fact that time spent on "people" issues and questions frustrates team members who prefer focusing on data, things, or action. Increasing frustration has nothing to do with your competence as a facilitative leader. Balancing human emotions and concerns with task accomplishment is your job.
31. When the team is stuck, ask the team to engage in a moment of silence to think through emotions the issue provokes and what the team should consider about the issue.
32. Don't say "any more ideas?" when the group has wound down after an active discussion. They feel compelled to add an idea and it just lengthens the meeting. Better to say: "Have you concluded this activity?"
33. Watch out for paying too much attention to the dominators and disrupters. Change physical position and pay attention to the productive members of the team. Don't try to placate the dominators too frequently. Totally ignore the rambler and encourage the team to do so through your modeling.

34. Don't try to make everyone happy. It gives disruptive members control of the group.
35. Move to the other side of the easel to where a dominant member sits — showing your back to him/her usually dampens the participation.
36. Picking on a facilitator leader about misspellings on the flipchart can signify anger about something else. The individual may feel ignored or steamrolled.
37. When someone wants to take a break at an important time, say: "You can take your break as you feel it is needed" and continue with the agenda discussion. Don't cater to the disrupter's agenda.
38. Language can signal how much conflict is occurring in a team. Differing interpretations of words such as stakeholder, beneficiary, customer, "real" customer, end user, champion, sponsor, and arguing over the right definition can consume many meetings. The issue is not definition of terms — the issue is who is going to have control over whom in the team.
39. Looking for the one best way to do something can be a trap. The team doesn't get the task done because there is often no one best way, so they continue to argue about it. The outcome is that nothing is decided, each person is free to do his or her "own thing," and no one is accountable because agreement could not be reached. Remind them they are working on business, process, procedural, or administrative problems — not designing/building a nuclear device! In these situations, there are "more effective ways" and "less effective ways" and not just one way.
40. Be sure to write down "inappropriate" comments verbatim. Don't edit or whitewash the comment. Some folks are not politically astute, so give them pause for thought by putting their publicly stated views in writing. Don't scratch the comment unless the whole group agrees it ought to be marked off. This is one time you ignore the author's request to black it out. He/she said it and it's time to own it.
41. Don't show your tension by tapping the marker on your hand,

rolling your neck from side to side, or looking at your watch frequently.
42. Don't ever try to convince a team to do something. That's managerial behavior, and, unfortunately, it's not trusted.
43. By the same token, don't "sell" someone on why a facilitative leader would be useful.
44. When co-facilitating, don't have the observer sit with the team. The observing facilitator should sit beside and a little behind the flipchart or in some other out-of-the-way location.
45. If possible, do not summarize the team's conclusions or accomplishments at the close of a session. Have the participants do it. At closing, it is appropriate to make observations about their progress and their team dynamics — things they would not be aware of until pointed out.

The Essence of Facilitative Leadership

As a facilitative leader you cannot avoid bringing who you are to what you do. You are the instrument of change and the most powerful aspect of facilitation. After all, you cannot lead unless others are willing to follow! Followers determine who leads and who doesn't when it comes to "out of the box" leadership.

Remember: The more you know yourself, the more centered you are, and the more you are willing to share yourself, the more the team will benefit. When you are authentic, sincere in wanting to serve, self disclose, openly and honestly tell it like it is in a sincere and caring way, leading as a facilitative leader will serve both you and the team.

About Linda Logan-Condon

*L*inda Logan-Condon is President of LTD Unlimited, an international training and development company. Linda is recognized for her work in exceptional leadership, team excellence, collaborative change, and professional coaching. Her clients include Intel Corporation, GAP, Nortel, Capital One, Lucent Technology, MatrixOne, AmeriCredit, Sandia National Laboratory, Sprint PCS, Honeywell, AT&T, and Johnson & Johnson. In addition, she has international clients in South Africa, India, and Russia. Internationally, Linda is a well-known speaker and author. She is specifically known for her presentations for the American Society of Training and Development, the International Society for Performance and Instruction, and the Society of Human Resource Management. Most recently, Linda was the kick-off speaker for the Executive Coaching Track at the International Coaches Federation Conference where she presented on, "The Power of Leadership: Vision, Integrity, and Action."

Contact Information:
Linda Logan-Condon
LTD Unlimited
11728 Linn Avenue NE
Albuquerque, NM 87123
Phone: (505) 292-8015
Fax: (505) 293-5270
E-mail: lloganc@flash.net
Website: www.ltdunlimited.com

LINKS TO LEADERSHIP

by Michele Matt, CSP and Steve Rutledge

"Perhaps the only true mystery to golf is the essential magnetism the game possesses which makes so many of us, regardless of discouragement, never quite turn in our trench coats and magnifying glasses and stop our search for answers."

— Ben Hogan

You may have heard the story about the junior executive who walks into her boss's office and says, her voice full of frustration, "I've mastered all aspects of my job and I'm consistently at the top of the performance scale. Tell me, what else does a person have to do to get ahead around here?" Her boss hands her a set of golf clubs and says, "Here, master these."

The story, with a touch of humor, illustrates the growing connection between business and golf. A recent survey of senior-level business executives concluded at a consensus opinion that playing golf with someone is a good way to learn about a person's character, competitiveness and motivation. Every day, on countless golf courses around the world, business associates are evaluated, relationships forged, and deals made. Golf has truly become the recreational activity of choice in the business world.

The punch line of the story also makes the point that golf is an extremely difficult game. As the quote at the beginning of this chapter explains, even Ben Hogan, the best golfer of his time, understood that even though he might spend a lifetime consumed by the quest for improvement, the game of golf was one that could never be perfected. How many of us feel the same about our leadership abilities? Are we always searching for the right strategy or most innovative technique to improve our effectiveness as a leader . . . whether it's in our jobs, at home, or in the community?

Like golf, leadership can never be mastered. However, the goal of this chapter is to identify the qualities shared by the world's greatest golfers and "link" them to the qualities exhibited by the most successful leaders. Perhaps the easiest way to do that is to ask, "What makes the best, the best?" Obviously, the best golfers have superior physical skills, but we believe it's also what they have within their hearts and minds. We believe they think, feel, and act in a manner that sets them apart from the competition.

Thanks to the soaring popularity of the game and cable television, professional golfers are on display each week. We can watch and learn. Too bad the board meetings or strategic planning sessions of corporate leaders like Jack Welch or Bill Gates aren't televised. It would be interesting to watch them struggle with the difficulties of their "game."

Tiger Woods, the best golfer of our time and a major reason millions of people have recently become drawn to the game, shares Ben Hogan's view, when he said *"I think I will continue to learn how to play this game until the day I die. It always changes. You always will learn. That's one of the great things about it."*

We agree with Ben and Tiger that excellence, wherever it may be found, manifests itself in a person's desire to continuously learn and grow. This passion for the "game" and the pursuit of excellence are the same qualities that drive also a common quality amongst successful leaders.

In this chapter we will explore our theory that, generally speaking, both golfers and leaders are challenged by the need to successfully manage the ***People*** they depend upon, the ***Attitude*** of those people, as well as their own, and the ***Resources*** available in order to effectively execute their game plan. In other words, both successful golfers and leaders must manage *P.A.R.* — ***People, Attitude, and Resources.***

Managing People

"What makes a great captain? Twelve great players. My job is to get them matched up and motivate them so they make me look good. If they play great, we all look great. If they don't, I look dumb."
— Curtis Strange, 2002 Ryder Cup Captain

Managing **People** begins with the recognition that whether it's the game of golf or leadership, you can't do it all yourself. As Captain Curtis suggests, select the right people for your team, clarify their responsibilities, help them work well together, and then allow them to perform their jobs.

Whether in golf or leadership, the process of building a team begins with an assessment of your own strengths and weaknesses. Although there isn't a pat formula for managing people, one winning strategy is to lead with your strengths and delegate to your weaknesses. Identify those areas of responsibility where you need the most support and find team members that have those particular skills and talents. Successful leaders seek the wisdom of experts to enhance their performance and results. A leader must possess the self-confidence to recognize that asking for help shows strength of character, not weakness.

Implicit in the above quote from Curtis Strange is also the suggestion that a leader is responsible for providing an environment that fosters superior performance from the entire team. Tiger acknowledges, *"Everything I have learned in this game I've basically learned from somebody else. They've given me that knowledge, and it's my responsibility to pass that on and share that knowledge."* He's not just talking about swinging a golf club; he's talking about a philosophy of managing relationships and sharing what he has learned to help others. He's talking about empowering leadership . . . sharing knowledge to bring out the best in everyone.

What is Tiger's formula for managing his people? We can assume he realizes that his primary responsibility is to play golf to the best of his ability. Cognizant of the fact that improvement is always possible, Tiger asked Butch Harmon, one of the most respected teaching pros in the game, to be his coach. He then recruited one of the best caddies,

Steve Williams. There isn't a player on tour who wouldn't appreciate having Steve by their side. The role of a caddie, a good caddie, can be much more than just a bag carrier. A caddie can also serve as an advisor, assistant coach, and even a psychologist at times. Steve has those capabilities and has proven to be an excellent match for Tiger.

Do you have a "coach," Who is or could be your "coach"? Someone to help you learn and strive for improvement? Do you have a "caddie," someone who will give you honest feedback? They may be called mentors or consultants in the business world, but you get the idea. Most effective leaders rely on such people to support and advise them.

The best golfers realize there are other aspects of their life, beyond golf, that need tending while they focus on their golf game. For instance, managing financial and business transactions. The people responsible for these areas may not be as visible as a coach or a caddie, but they are critical members of the team and must be highly competent as well. Ray Kroc, founder of McDonald's, believed, *"You're only as good as the people you hire."*

First-rate people hire first-rate people; second-rate people hire *third-rate* people. In order to attract the best people, leaders must create a work environment that motivates and brings out the best of each team member.

Is your team first rate? Have you created a working atmosphere that makes people want to be a part of your team?

A good leader will create an environment of shared goals, an environment that promotes relationships in which knowledge is shared and learning encouraged, where everyone strives to improve not only themselves but also the team as a whole.

Communication is key to any relationship. Share your knowledge with your team and ask the same of them. Make sure everyone understands what is expected of them, and give them ongoing feedback on their performance, and recognize their accomplishments. Ben Hogan believed, *"You don't simply tell a player what he is doing wrong. That's not much help. You must explain to him what he ought to be doing, why it is correct, and the result it produces — and work like blazes to get it across so that he really understands what you are talking about."*

Studies consistently reveal that the leading reason for poor performance is poor communication.

If the world's best golfers had no coach to learn from, no caddie to help shoulder the burdens, and no one to do any of the other work, they'd never win a tournament. But by properly managing their people, they have the expertise, team support, and knowledge to achieve great success. The same applies to a leader of any endeavor. When the right people are in the right positions doing the right things the right way, the whole team wins!

Managing Attitude

"A golfer can and must decide how he will think."

— Bob Rotella,
author of *Golf is Not a Game of Perfect*

One of the most impressive performances ever on a golf course took place at the 2000 US Open at Pebble Beach. Tiger Woods ultimately won this tournament by 15 shots, the largest margin of victory in the 100-year history of the US Open. Although Tiger thoroughly dominated the tournament from start to finish, the way he played the final round and, in particular, his final hole, was especially fascinating. Not so much due to the physical skills displayed, although he really did put on a whale of a show, but more so for his ***Attitude*** about how to play the game.

As Tiger stood on the tee of the 72nd and final hole of the tournament, he needed a birdie to break the record for the lowest score ever recorded in a US Open. Arguably the most spectacular finishing hole in golf, the par five 18th at Pebble Beach is a perfect blend of risk and reward, offering players willing to risk a long shot over the water, the potential to reach the green in two and the chance to make an easy birdie.

So there he stood, one hole to play and 15 shots ahead of his closest competitor. The opportunity to write his name on one more page of the history books was there for the taking. There was no way he would not pull out the big dog and go for it.

At least that's what we thought, but, instead, we watched, confounded, as Steve Williams, Tiger's caddie, handed him an iron, not the driver. Tiger had chosen to play safe by hitting an iron off the tee, then another iron up the fairway, virtually eliminating the risk of splashing his ball, leaving a short iron to the green where he two-putted for his par. As a result, he tied the record but did not break it. What the . . . was he thinking? Why didn't he go for it?

Tiger played the last hole the way he did because he had set his own goal before the final round began. His goal was to make nothing worse than par on any hole. As he stood on the 18th tee his scorecard was filled with pars or better on each of the first 17 holes. A par on the last and he would achieve *his* goal and still tie the record. And that's exactly what he did. An interesting attitude, don't you think?

Attitude is a combination of many things. Confidence (not ego), evaluating risk, decision making, and perseverance are among the most important factors that contribute to attitude. Attitude is a decision to think in a certain way. As the quote from Bob Rotella suggests, *leaders* must decide how they will think.

Both successful golfers and leaders demonstrate confidence. We've no doubt that when Tiger began his final round of the US Open he was extremely confident in his ability to perform at the level necessary to achieve his goals. That was the attitude he had chosen. This confidence requires good decision-making, judgment and risk taking. Successful leaders are capable of evaluating a situation, a condition or state of position, determining the desired end-result, and maintaining the confidence necessary to achieve the goal. Leaders exude confidence, but they do so without letting ego influence their attitude or their actions.

Leaders make decisions. It's part of the job description. And every decision involves risk. Yes or no, stop or go, change or do nothing; every decision can lead to success or failure. A good leader has to determine which course of action provides the best opportunity to accomplish the goal. Evaluating risk and making decisions go hand in hand, in golf or leadership.

When challenged by the environment, it's easy to allow negative thoughts and fear to stifle one's potential for success. Tiger's goal of completing his final round with nothing worse than pars on his scorecard was not accomplished without fighting through some adversity. The strength and perseverance of attitude determines ability to overcome the obstacles in the way of a positive performance.

In Michele's best-selling book, *Attitude: The Choice is Yours*, she suggests people listen to the "self talk" that channels their thoughts, feelings, and actions. Paying close attention to the voice within us will tell us things we believe we can or can't do. Even though the odds may be against them, successful leaders or golfers are able to control what they believe they can achieve.

Managing your attitude can bring positive results, both on and off the golf course. Remember, you decide how you will think and manage those thoughts. Attitude is a choice!

Managing Resources

"All fourteen are my favorites. If they are not my favorites, they are not in the bag."

— Tiger Woods,
when asked which club was his favorite

This section was the most difficult for us to write, simply because the definition of resources can be difficult to quantify. If you think about it, nearly everything that helps a business operate could be called a resource. So in order to simplify our discussion we have divided resources into three categories: intellectual resources such as information and people, physical resources such as equipment, and limited resources such as time and money.

Professional golfers might consider their coach or the statistics available on their performance as intellectual resources and their clubs as a physical resource. With time and money as the assets used to acquire these intellectual and physical resources.

The use of time and money is the same in the business world and, since both are limited, managing resources becomes a balancing act. Successful leaders must formulate a strategy for managing, utilizing, and developing resources.

In golf the term "course management" refers to the process of developing a game plan for playing a particular golf course. In business, the analogous term is "project management." Throughout the implementation of a "management" strategy, in golf or business, decisions are constantly being made to maximize performance and assure proper utilization of the resources available.

Inherent in this process is the point Tiger makes in his quote above. If he lacks confidence in a particular club, he won't use it. That club will simply become dead weight for Steve to carry around in the bag. Although Tiger is talking about his clubs, the same applies to any resource. If there is a lack of confidence in the ability of a resource to perform, that resource will become dead weight that must be supported by other resources, reducing their performance in the process.

A tournament golfer is allowed to choose and carry only 14 clubs and to use one caddie during any given round of golf. There are times when, for strategic reasons related to course management, a player will replace one or more clubs between rounds. On rare occasions, a player will even replace a caddie (remember "Fluff," Tiger's first caddie?). Having the proper resources to do your best is imperative to the success of both golfers and leaders.

One of the most important intellectual resources both golfers and leaders can use to identify areas that need attention are statistics, especially those that measure performance. The most obvious and significant measures in golf are the number of tournaments won, the rankings on the money list, and scoring statistics. Naturally, each round's score is the core number that interests the fans and motivates the players.

Beyond these obvious measures, golf has more statistics than you can imagine. The Professional Golfers Association maintains information on driving distance and accuracy, greens in regulation, sand saves, and number of putts, just to name a few. Therefore, golfers can study every facet of their performance, allowing them to easily identify areas that require additional attention in order to improve and set goals.

In business, the obvious and significant measures are income growth, profitability, and return on equity. But not all businesses have accurate measurements for the more intangible elements of their operation, such as customer service and satisfaction, marketing effectiveness, and others. It is in this area that business leaders can take a page from golf. They may need to develop and manage ways to measure the more detailed aspects of resource performance since, just as in golf, these details ultimately drive the achievement possible in the more significant areas of performance.

This process of breaking the "game" into smaller pieces is an integral part of the management strategies we spoke of earlier, course management in golf and project management in business. In golf, course management starts with an assessment of the golf course as a whole in order to define the basic pieces of the game plan. From there, each of the 18 holes is analyzed separately to determine the best strategy for each hole and, finally, even individual shots are planned so that the golfer will be in the best position for the next shot. Sometimes the plan has to be changed; after all, golfers do hit bad shots. But that's the idea.

This is the same concept corporate leaders use in project management. Once the overall goal is defined and resources selected to accomplish that goal, a leader will break that goal into smaller pieces, frequently defined in time (monthly, quarterly, etc.) and by segments. In this way, the process of selecting and managing resources is simplified, and the team also gets a psychological lift since each of the smaller tasks appears much more manageable.

Clearly, managing resources is a difficult and complex task. But when someone asks, "How are you doing?," if you can describe your performance in specific measures rather than just in general terms, your results will be moving in the right direction. No matter which "game" you play, performance is directly tied to the appropriate selection and proper management of resources.

Our Link to Leadership

"The most important achievement is always the next *one. ."*
— Steve Rutledge

Have you ever replayed a round of golf in your head without feeling like you could have done better? When did you shoot your best ever score? Don't you still try to beat it? The best leaders, just like the best golfers, never stop striving for success. They never lose the desire to compete or the passion for achievement.

Past accomplishments are just that, past. There is always another step to take along the fairway of life. Another vision that stirs the soul and provides another goal to pursue. The process never ends. But then again, it wouldn't be any fun if it did.

"Do what you do best, better than the rest."
— Michele Matt, CSP

Whether I'm on the golf course or managing my business, I have found the most efficient way to get the most desirable results is to focus my energies on what I can do, both mentally and physically. Everyone is unique in thoughts, words, and action. In order to be true to yourself and those around you, take time to understand yourself and what inspires you to excellence. Vince Lambardi, legendary coach of the Green Bay Packers, believed that *"The quality of a person's life is in direct proportion to their commitment to excellence, regardless of their chosen field of endeavor."*

We hope this chapter has given you insight and suggestions for managing your "game of life" on and off the golf course. It matters not what you do, but how you do something that ultimately leads to what you get out of life. Realize that in order to make a positive impact at work, home, or play you need to be effective at managing P.A.R.: the People you rely upon and influence, the Attitude that channels your action and the Resources available to achieve desired results.

Keep swinging and enjoy your "game"!

About Michele Matt, CSP & Steve Rutledge

*M*ichele Matt, CSP, is the founder and owner of Inspiring Solutions, a company that works with leaders who want to develop their strategic plan and motivate their people. She is a best-selling author of several books, videos and training resources. Each year this 'Attitude Adjuster' speaks to over 100 different groups at conferences, businesses, schools, and even prisons. In addition, Michele facilitates a 10-step strategic planning process for company leaders. She is a nationally recognized, award-winning leader in several organizations such as the National Speakers Association and American Society of Training & Development. Michele has been swinging a golf club since age 5 and has won several team and individual tournaments, including the Des Moines Mercedes Championship in 2001.

In 2002, Steve Rutledge became President, CEO and Chairman of the Board at Farmers Mutual Hail Insurance Company of Iowa. During his career, which spans more than 30 years in insurance and reinsurance, he has served on several boards, including two industry associations, the National Crop Insurance Service, and the Crop Insurance Research Bureau. Steve has also been a frequent speaker at various conferences and seminars. Most recently, he was chosen to serve on the National Task Force on Corporate Governance by the National Association of Mutual Insurance Companies. Among his golf accomplishments are three holes-in-one, including one at St. Andrews in Scotland. He currently carries an 8 handicap at his home course, Des Moines Golf & Country Club, site of the 1999 US Senior Open.

Contact Information:

Michele Matt
Inspiring Solutions
2709 Scenic Place
West Des Moines, IA 50265
Phone: (515) 225-1249
Fax: (515) 225-9396
E-mail:
  Michele@InspiringSolutions.com
Website: www.InspiringSolutions.com

Steve Rutledge
Farmers Mutual Hail Insurance Co.
2323 Grand Avenue
Des Moines, IA 50312
Phone: (515) 237-7318
Fax: (515) 237-7397
E-mail: steve@fmh.com

Getting to the Finish Line

by Drew Stevens

The challenges facing businesses today grow out of a globalized economy, which creates both more hazards and opportunities for everyone and forces firms to make dramatic improvements, not only to compete and prosper but also to merely survive. Globalization, in turn, is being driven by a broad and powerful set of forces associated with technological change, international economic integration, domestic market maturation within the more developed countries, and the collapse of worldwide communism. No one is immune to these forces. Even companies that sell only in small geographic regions feel the impact of globalization.

These changes in business require changes in management and business processes. Some of these changes are explicit, such as a switch from paper to electronic. And some are implicit, such as roles and titles. One noticeable change involves managers learning about and trying to become leaders. Today, the concepts of "leadership" and "innovation" are replacing those of "management" and "conformity," and, in the 21st century, savvy companies are replacing their managers with leaders. Substituting "leadership" and "leader" for "management" and "manager" are not just new-age word games. They are the linchpins of any enterprise in today's global marketplace.

What, then, is a manager? A leader? Are they the same person? Can they be? Does one precede the other? Can one be a manager and not a leader? Can one be a leader and not a manager? Finally, are the differences subtle or are there vast contrasts?

Management and Leadership Defined

Management	Leadership
Planning and budgeting	Establishing direction
Organizing and staffing	Aligning people
Controlling and problem solving	Motivating and inspiring
Produces a degree of predictability and order	Producing change, often to a dramatic degree

Managers

Managers are people who get things done. Give them a task and a mission and they will complete it. There is no need for strategy as managers react tactically to environmental and corporate goals.

A manager is similar to the quarterback of a football team. He ensures that people align themselves correctly on the field and run the designed patterns. The quarterback or manager ensures that all know their place and get the assigned job completed. The leader or head coach designs the plays and creates a team environment by preparing and planning, yet all execution is completed by the quarterback.

Webster's dictionary describes management as: 1) the act or art of managing: the conducting or supervising of something (as a business) 2) judicious use of means to accomplish an end 3) the collective body of those who manage or direct an enterprise.

A manager ensures the success of policies, procedures and practices. A manager is not concerned with feelings, team spirit, or employees. In fact, the manager is concerned only with project and task completion, nothing more. A manager is apathetic to employees and roles and focuses only on the beginning and the end of a particular effort.

Leaders

In contrast with management, leadership is a complex process by which a person influences others to accomplish a mission, task, or objective and directs the organization in a way that makes it more cohesive and coherent. A person carries out this process by applying her leadership attributes (e.g., beliefs, values, ethics, character, knowledge, and skills). Although the position of manager, supervisor or leader gives a person the authority to accomplish certain tasks and objectives in the organization, this power does not make anyone a leader . . . it simply makes a person the boss. Leadership makes people want to achieve high goals and objectives, while, on the other hand, bosses tell people to accomplish a task or objective.

Leadership is tricky business. Depending on the environment, the circumstances, and the problems and objectives, different qualities are required for an individual to be a successful leader.

Leadership can be quantified as having two primary purposes: to inspire innovation and creativity, and to motivate participation and achievement. And — as opposed to management — leadership provides omnidirectional benefits.

A successful leader midway in the chain of command in an organization can inspire and motivate employees, staff members, and co-managers. Inspiration and motivation are dynamic terms, and the energy, aura, and environment produced by strong leadership affect all with whom the leader interacts.

A unified mission, shared aspirations, and universal goals and values are essential for strong, successful leadership to flourish. An individual who cannot enter an environment of disorder, discord, drift, fear, aimlessness, confusion, mistrust, or paranoia, and coalesce a united team with a purpose, direction, objective, and a good feeling about itself, is not a leader.

A successful leader understands how to interact with people; he or she is involved in relationships. The leader creates a sense in each co-worker that everyone can make a difference. The leader builds a team based on human relations and human strengths.

To be a successful leader, one must know how to choose good managers who can be effective with delegated responsibilities. Not recognizing this need for dependence upon those with different talents has caused some of the most brilliant leaders to briefly excite their world only to fizzle like a burned-out firecracker, leaving no foundation for a lasting success.

Managers must be detail oriented to be successful; leaders must be concept oriented, able to see the big picture. Good leaders usually dislike details; good managers may have a hard time seeing beyond them. Of course, there are exceptions to this: There are effective managers with leadership ability and leaders with good management ability. But the more undistracted devotion we can give to our strongest talents, the more effective we will be.

Being too involved with details makes it hard to see the big picture. It is just as hard to keep a good handle on the details and see the big picture at the same time. The most effective leadership comes from a partnership of those who lead and those who manage — a partnership that allows each to concentrate on his or her own role.

The advancement system in a typical hierarchy, which is the structure of almost every human enterprise, makes it hard for someone with good leadership qualities to rise to a position of leadership. The lower echelons of a hierarchy usually reward management skills more than leadership. A leader will rarely be good enough at the managerial skills required for advancement within the system, unless he devotes himself to the quality that will be most needed when he does come to his place of leadership — discipline.

The detail-oriented management skills, which may be foreign to his nature, must be understood by the leader if he is to interact effectively with those whose work will be essential to his success as a leader. The typical hierarchy will be most difficult for even a great leader to advance in, but those who do advance will be those best prepared for their task.

Even if it is tedious and boring, the potential leader should see hierarchy as a cocoon. It is the great struggle required by the butterfly to get out of its cocoon that strengthens it so it can use those great wings. It will be the potential leader's struggle to get to the top of the hierarchy, which serves as preparation for the great responsibility of leadership.

Almost every great enterprise was founded by a leader, not a manager. But almost every enterprise that lives past its founder is taken over by a manager. There are two basic reasons for this phenomenon:

1) There are so few leaders who can make it through the gauntlet of the hierarchy.
2) Most leaders are poor managers and fail to understand the need for a partnership with managers.

Therefore, the enterprise will be in desperate need of a manager at the top for a while. When the manager first takes over, profitability and efficiency will usually increase for a period of time, but progress under the manager type will be invariably slow, jeopardizing future success.

A manager looks at what is; a leader is always looking at what can be. It takes both qualities to get the full picture; either one without the other is ultimately doomed to mediocrity or failure. If managers understood leadership and leaders understood management, there would almost certainly be far less decline in enterprise, and both leadership and management would be more effective.

The leader's job is to give the managers direction, vision, and inspiration. Regardless of how good the leader is, he or she will be ineffective without good managers. Degrees of success or failure will be determined by the quality of managers.

In addition to flexibility and vision, the leader must have the ability to develop and articulate a value proposition, to maintain it in a dynamic market, to energize others to buy into it and to commit to a culture that values mentorship and learning. It will be the learning organization that makes change easier and assists in creative production and harmony. The would-be leaders who are unwilling or unable to demonstrate these leadership behaviors will find themselves with few followers.

Success Leadership the GE Way

Exemplifying the leadership success of GE and Jack Welch, several principles create a difference between the managed and the led organization. Jack Welch is famous for his leadership appeal. He does not believe in the hierarchical approach or bureaucracy. He feels all companies must be led to become global icons. Further, he believes that a led organization is a motivated organization. In his most recent book, Jack Welch describes three areas that exemplify how to create a motivated workforce through true leadership.

- A learning culture
- De-layer the management
- Turn employees into owners

Create a learning culture

In his acclaimed book *Get Better or Get Beaten,* Jack Welch depicts the importance of a learning organization. Mr. Welch indicates that the key to a leading organization is to teach the troops a process, which ultimately produces higher motivation and team spirit. Welch states, "Shared knowledge would provide a competitive advantage and that advantage would translate into higher annual growth rates." Further, Welch notes, "This boundarylessness learning culture killed any view that assumed GE was the only way, or even the best way. The operative assumption today is that someone, somewhere has a better idea, and the operative compulsion is to find out who has that better idea, learn it, and put it into action — fast." For Welch, a learning culture enables employees to wear the "Badge of Honor." The kudos motivate employees to express themselves and affirm that they are acknowledged, accepted, and required for the operation's existence. An organization that creates learning creates leadership, not just from the top down but from within the heart and soul of the individual employee.

De-layer the organization

The antithesis of bureaucracy, GE under Welch decided there was too much management. Welch feels that too much management slows down decisions, creates administrative quagmires, and demoralizes employee empowerment. Similar to a learning organization, GE placed certain decision making into the hands of the employees. The benefit to GE was faster decisions, motivation from empowerment, better profits, and more efficiency.

Welch states, "Big corporations are filled with people in bureaucracy who want to cover things — cover the bases, say they did everything a little bit. Well, now we have people out there all by themselves, there they are, accountable for their successes and their failures. But it gives them a chance to flourish. Now you will see some wilt. That's the sad part of the job. Some who looked good in big bureaucracy looked silly when you left them alone."

Turn employees into owners

By enabling each employee to become CEO of his or her professional life, GE provided an environment where ideas can be shared, people can learn, and employees matter. The way to develop more productive employees and create a competitive spirit is to unleash the power of the individual. Welch feels that by turning an employee loose to run within the company, fresh ideas and innovation flow on a daily basis. It is from this process that productivity and profitability increase.

Motivation within the corporate setting is difficult. The people must respect each other in order to become effective as a team and produce the necessary work. Management practices are not concerned with people — their feelings, their desires. Leadership practices are concerned with people's feelings, people's motivation, and employee interaction. While management focuses on process and procedure, leadership stresses professionalism and personal development. GE exemplifies the difference between a leadership-designed organization — one in which a person can flourish from employees and a management designed organization. *From Get Better or Get Beaten*, two quotes between leadership and management, 1) on leadership and motivation, "For 25 years you've paid for my hands when you could have had my brain — for nothing," 2) Management, "We spent 90 percent of our time on the floor figuring out how to screw the management, and that was okay because you guys spent 95 percent of the time figuring out how to screw us."

Welch's kudos aren't from being a leader but from building a dedicated and passionate workforce on respect, empowerment, and motivation. He certainly could have maintained the process management; however, GE would not be as profitable nor one of America's most admired corporations. Clearly, GE exemplifies differences, not only in management and leadership but of motivation and efficiency. By respecting employees, making them a part of the team, and being mindful of their attitudes and aptitudes, GE has built a house of leadership. After all, take a look at many of America's current CEO's. These individuals are now building the next phases of leadership and possibly the next GE's.

The new millennium signals a new beginning for society and for corporations. The new millennium brings with it a transformation of management to leadership. This change creates a renewal of management practices and the birth of new leaders. Clearly, the new millennium is about change. Business must change to become powerful, profitable, and proficient.

Employees of the 21st century are looking for guidance and for leaders with a vision who can take them into unchartered waters but navigate as if they have been there many times. Leaders must have vision, leaders must have faith, and leaders must ask and answer the difficult questions. The answers to these will come through trial and error and good experiential education. Certainly, without learning and without knowledge, leaders fail, but with the proper guidance and education, future leaders are born.

There is a clear distinction between managers and leaders. However, a manager can grow to become a leader. I am not convinced that leaders are born as much as they are born with a quality that, through the practice of management, develops over time. I believe that corporations need both roles to be effective, yet it is imperative to switch from a process oriented organization to one of leadership. Why? I believe employees are in need of direction, mentoring, and spirit. True managers are apathetic to these needs and their attitude shows in reduced corporate productivity. Leading organizations like GE build teams, create spirit, and bring cohesion where division previously existed.

About Drew Stevens

*D*rew Stevens is all about results. He has delivered results on sales, productivity and profitability since starting his business, Getting to the Finish Line, in 1999. His passionate and personable presence and his easy to remember ideas such as C4, BE ALERT and ABLE create immediate efficiency and effectiveness. Drew speaks and consults internationally and he is frequently called upon by the media for his expertise. He stays current with memberships in the National Speakers Association and American Society of Training and Development.

Contact Information:
Drew Stevens
Getting to the Finish Line
627 Thorntree Lane
Eureka, St. Louis, MO 63025
Phone: (636) 938-4486
Phone: (toll free) (877) 391-6821
E-mail: drew@gettingtothefinishline.com
Website: www.gettingtothefinishline.com

Power Etiquette: Leadership Skills that Open Doors Money Cannot

by Dana May Casperson

Power Etiquette skills begin deep inside you. They begin with your values, your ethics, and your feelings about yourself and others. Your actions reflect how you feel about yourself and your life goals. This is not cerebral stuff but common sense. Your leadership skills should be practiced every day so that they become second nature to you, allowing you to be confident and competent in your daily tasks and job. It is true that some leaders are born leaders like alpha dogs; others can learn the skills to be more organized and outward focused. However, not all people can be leaders. We have genetic inheritance, which provides the talents. We need to define and refine them.

Think of yourself as a professional package, like a gift. The more interesting the outside wrapping, the more people will want to see inside and to know more about you. You have the power to be attractive just by being interesting and comfortable to be around. That is magnetic appeal. Power Etiquette skills are the professional tools which make you the magnet for other people to want to be around you and learn from you. They can be thought of as your three V's to success — visual, verbal, and virtual.

Visual is what people see. What people see is what they perceive you to be. This perception includes your wardrobe, gestures, and body language. We live in a visual-byte culture where we make judgements in 2-4 seconds. That impression is lasting, and rarely do we have an opportunity to make another one. So, why not make the first impression superb?

Verbal is all that a person hears from you — your verbal communication and your voice messages.

Virtual is everything about you that does not include your presence or voice, such as your written communication on paper and on screen.

Look deeper at the three V's.

Your visual impression is what I call your visual resumé. What people see tells all about you, your respect for them, how you feel at that given moment or day, and how competent you are in the situation.

How to polish the rough edges is what Power Etiquette is all about. This is an ongoing learning process. Some skills change with the level of professional responsibility and some behavior expectations change with the times. Each decade produces subtle changes in dress, communication, and how we conduct our business. Always keep in mind that when change is needed, ask yourself if these changes are congruent with your value system and beliefs. As a leader you guide the direction of the organization, association, group, or business. The responsibility resides with the leader. You set the tone for procedures and success. Never compromise solely for money. The decision to do so can easily be the ruin of the company.

Your wardrobe is an important part of your visual impression, so plan your clothing for optimum visual impact. You need to:

1. Plan your wardrobe just as you make a business plan. Coordinate your wardrobe by color and style to include four trousers/skirts and pants (four total); four button-front and polo shirts, five ties/four blouses and sweaters; four jackets and sweater jackets. This combination can be maximized to more than forty different outfits.

   I call this the "4 + 4 + 4 = 40 formula."

   - Maximize every possible combination of clothing.
   - Maintain your wardrobe.
   - Update it each year with new color or style.
   - Make certain the garments fit.

- Determine that the clothing is appropriate for your body type and work situation.
2. Check your body language. Make sure that it matches your words or you sabotage your message.
   - Do you stand tall?
   - Do you drag your feet?
   - Do you lean on walls and desks when you stand?
3. Your gestures should be appropriate for the situation and location.
   Eliminate distracting gestures like:
   - Pushing up your glasses.
   - Throwing your hair over you shoulder.
   - Rubbing your earlobe.
   - Sucking through your front teeth.
   - Biting your nails.
   - Chewing on hair.
   - Twisting your mustache.
   - Jangling coins and keys in trouser pockets.
4. The maintenance of your teeth, nails, hair, and clothing should be impeccable.
   - Shoes should be polished and in good repair.
   - Tattoos should be covered.
   - Change hairstyle every few years.
   - Hair should be secured back if it is longer than shoulder length.
   - Nails should be clean and buffed.
   - Make-up should be in moderation.
   - Not more than two earrings on each side.
   - Hems and cuffs should be intact and not frayed.
   - Facial hair, if allowed, should be trimmed and shaped.

Verbal

One kind word can last a lifetime. You can make a difference through what you say or do not say. One sentence of well-chosen words can change the entire direction of someone's career. However, keep in mind that what you think you say may not be what someone else hears. The old adage "say what you mean and mean what you say" refers to the power of credibility and competence. If you say it, mean it and do it. Never promise to do something you have no intention of doing. Your words need to be well chosen, meaningful, and respectful. Avoid slang and swear words. Keep your industry lingo to office conversations; others may not know what you are talking about.

Your words must mirror your body language or you destroy your credibility. Slouchy posture and loud, rapid speaking are not congruent. Get in touch with your visual and verbal messages to align them for power.

All speaking is public speaking because whenever you speak, someone is listening. If your leadership position requires speaking more frequently or to large audiences, you might choose to work with a coach or join a Toastmasters® group to ease your fears and improve your speaking delivery. Remember that everyone can benefit from coaching to fine-tune his or her speaking style.

Your voice messages are part of your verbal resumé. The outgoing message should be energetic and informative. If you do not frequently change it, call yourself and check your outgoing message. Try changing it every month if you do not make a daily message change.

When you leave a voice message be certain that it includes:

1. Your name and phone number.
2. Your reason for calling.
3. Your message.
4. Your name and phone number.

By leaving your name and phone number at the beginning and end of the message, you help the listener get the number correctly, reinforce your name, and eliminate the need to listen again to the message. Make it easy for the person to return your call. Speak slowly and clearly. Speak the numbers as though you are writing each one.

Smile when you speak; it "sounds" in your voice. Phone calls and e-messages should be returned within 48 hours. Be a powerful communicator by choosing clear, concise words. Your power comes from being understood.

Virtual

Virtual communication is all that we say and do on paper and with words on a screen without intonation or explanation. Any time you put a pen to paper or fingers to keyboard you are displaying your professional skills. Spellchecker does not correct everything. When you are sending correspondence — especially contracts, proposals, and letters — print them out, stand, and read aloud. Reading out loud helps find the errors not seen by sight-reading. Lucky you, if you have staff to read your outgoing correspondence. Most of us must take editing responsibilities, which are vital for professional communication. Errors occur, so be lenient of others to a point; but your credibility is assessed and measured by the reader on every piece of written communication. Spelling is not all there is to writing; word choice and grammar, capitalization and punctuation are key elements to good writing.

Technology made us available 24/7 or 12/5. There is ease in contacting people whenever and wherever they are. With that ability, we are faced with more challenges to respond. People make demands on our response time with their expectations of a quick answer. Technology such as e-mail, pagers, faxes, mobile phones, office phones, text messages on mobile phones, and instant messaging makes it possible to receive a higher volume of communication which, in turn, must be dealt with and managed in some way.

Instant messaging is rapidly becoming an office communication tool. Get ready for this technology because it will soon be part of many offices. IM, as it is called, is more intrusive than e-mail because a message box appears on the monitor screen. If several people are in IM communication with you, your screen could be covered with little boxes. IM software has not been perfected sufficiently for everyone's use, but indications are that IM will soon be commonplace in offices. Its use varies from customer service questions, to outside sales needing answers from the office, to interoffice communication with several people at once.

There is no end to the possibilities for virtual communication in the future. What we must determine is, how efficiently are we going to manage the demands? This decision takes conscious planning about how and when we are available and how rapidly we will respond.

Some people receive 200 e-mail messages daily. The reading and response time involved takes a significant amount of the workday and can undermine productivity.

Time management becomes the challenge for dealing with the demands made on your professional life. Leaders need to set the parameters for use, followed by discussion with staff on technology use in the office and employee rights for use of office software. These steps are crucial to productivity and competence. Magnetic leadership means polishing the three V's of power to master the art of leading others to greater productivity.

Now that you understand how vital your choices are for professional power, consider the following seventeen power tips. Work on improving yourself because these make the difference between normal and extraordinary leadership.

Seventeen tips to develop your magnetic style.

1. Get a grip

Your handshake speaks loudly about your confidence and competence. There is a special sense of connection when you shake hands with someone. To make it magnetic, practice with someone you trust. Get comments from both men and women because men shake hands differently with women than with men. You want to

- Position your feet so that you are facing the person.
- Look the person in the eye.
- Speak the person's name while shaking hands.
- Keep the hands vertical with thumb on top.

- Fit the hands web to web.
- Shake firmly, not softly.
- Shake 3-7 seconds.
- Shake hands often.
- Smile.

2. Be prepared

Carry your papers and briefcase in your left hand; thereby keeping your right hand free and ready to shake hands. If you get in the habit of keeping your right hand free of papers when you are out and about, especially in networking situations, you will always be ready to shake hands.

3. Make introductions

Your ease with introductions makes people feel comfortable around new acquaintances and provides small information bytes so that a conversation can continue beyond the hellos. Think of an introduction as a circle. When introducing two people:

- Speak the name of the highest-ranking person first.
- Use first and last names.
- Speak the names twice as you "make the circle."
- Mention a small bit of information about each person, but not too personal.
- Look at each person as you make the introduction.

"Cyndi Novak, I would like to introduce (or like you to meet) Heather Andrade, our HR director. Ms. Andrade, this is Ms. Novak, Project Manager for ABC Corporation. Heather recently vacationed in Hawaii and I think you also like to vacation there, Cyndi." The two now have a common thread of interest on which to begin a conversation.

If you are not sure who is the higher-ranking person, make the introduction anyway. It is better to say the wrong name first than not make an introduction at all.

A self-introduction is a 10-second or less statement about yourself and what you do. If you write this out in advance to make it clear and concise, then you can practice it. You can give a lot of information in a short time. Mention your name (first and last), your position, and the benefits of your business or service.

"Hello, my name is Dana May Casperson. I have a dual first name. I am an author and speaker on Magnetic Leadership, the Power Etiquette skills that open doors money cannot. My company provides your ticket to professional success."

4. Dress for respect

Plan your wardrobe so that it is respectful to yourself and the others you work with. This means that your choice of attire should be appropriate for your industry, geography, culture, time of day, season, your body shape and personal style.

5. Deliver what you promise

Be realistic about what you will do. If you say that you will send the report or make a recommendation, do it. There is nothing worse to discredit your credibility than to promise and not carry through. Your example for others serves as a model for them to do the same for you.

6. Answer it

Return e-mails and phone calls personally, if possible, as quickly as convenient and within 48 hours.

7. Acknowledge your co-workers

Every day
- Use the magic words of "Please," "Thank you," "I'm sorry," "Excuse me," "Hello" and "Goodbye."
- Acknowledge your co-workers through words: "I appreciate your effort." "Can you help me finish this project?"
- Show that you value your co-workers.
- Demonstrate respect to your co-workers by your actions and words.

8. Listen

Learn to ask questions and to listen for the answers. You learn more than you can imagine by asking and listening. The staff that is doing the unrecognized work has insight and knowledge that others do not. Spend time with them in the employee lounge and ask for their observations and opinions. You may be surprised by what they have observed and their insights into the company.

9. Make conversation an art

When you are informed and interesting to talk with, people will be attracted to you.

Learn by
- Reading and listening to the daily news.
- Reading weekly national news magazines.
- Knowing what is going on in your community.
- Being aware of what is happening in national sports.
- Going to the movies.
- Being able to recommend at least one current good movie.
- Knowing what books are on the best selling list.
- Reading outside your industry publications.

10. Be a gracious host

Learn the art of fine dining by knowing how to use the dining tools while conversing. Your credibility shines brightly at the dining table when you know how to make people feel at ease. Know how to guide the conversation when it goes off course, select easy-to-eat items off the menu, recognize all the tableware, (see illustration 1), handle the knife and fork correctly (illustration 2), and know when to close the conversation.

11. Use mobile phones thoughtfully

One quick way to polarize a potential client, client or colleague is to use your mobile while with them. Mobile phones are great tools of communication when used courteously. When in doubt, turn your mobile off. If you must take a call while with others, mention before the phone rings that you are expecting a call and ask if you may accept it. When the phone rings, get up and leave the room after you say "Hello," and before you begin the conversation.

Courteous mobile phone use includes:

- Turning it off during meetings (at meals, in offices, conferences, and home meetings).
- Turning it off during social events (concerts, plays, religious services, funerals and movies).
- Speaking softly when conversing.
- Not conducting job interviews, business deals, personnel issues.
- Moving to a quiet place away from others to converse.
- Choosing a non-intrusive ring tone.

12. Become an expert

Learn something well outside your profession. Develop an outside interest, which may involve community service, volunteering, or learning. To become magnetic and well educated you need to study outside your industry. Of course, the study may be a lifetime of learning.

Possible topics could include ones you already have a special interest in

- Foreign language
- Photography
- Old car restoration
- Painting
- Bicycling
- Travel
- Geography
- Winemaking
- Tea tasting
- Fishing
- Sailing
- Art

13. Get out of the rut

Know what is going on in your family, at their schools, and in the community. In order to stay up at the top of your profession, you need to know future as well as current industry trends.

Personally, you need small challenges to prod yourself to improve, refine, and grow. Make those small, incremental challenges to avoid

Travel opens the mind and helps us appreciate what we have. You may travel on weekends to local celebrations and events or plan annual or semi-annual trips to other countries. There is no doubt that traveling expands your interests and helps you to understand other ways to solve problems. For me, annual European bicycling trips expand my thinking, knowledge, and experience plus provide exercise.

16. Laugh a little
Develop a sense of humor to relieve the stress. It is always better to laugh at yourself and your mistakes. Never play tricks or tell jokes about others, especially co-workers and colleagues.

17. Smile
Smile often, even when you don't feel like it. Smiles are contagious and a smile relieves tension to make people feel more comfortable.

Magnetic leadership is more than directing people to be more productive; it is about modeling behavior that is thoughtful, creative, sincere, credible, competent and respectful. A leader provides a comfortable, caring environment in which others can express their concerns. When colleagues and co-workers feel valued and respected, they are more productive. The trickle down process works in even the shortest professional ladder. When the leader is thoughtful of others and values their expertise, they are, in turn, caring about those they work with.

Polish the three "V's" for success; then challenge yourself to the power tips that polish your professional leadership skills. Leadership is a continual growth line. As we face new situations, we can weather them. We just need to have a foundation of respectful attitude toward others and ourselves. From there, we must keep learning and improving ourselves because through the process we become better people to lead organizations and businesses. The magnetic field is created from the mix of talent and professional presence. You are a leader wherever you go.

Fill your professional package with interesting conversation, an expanse of knowledge, and then wrap it in a pleasing way. Your power comes from being fascinating, honest, highly ethical and caring. Continue to learn and modify your thinking because Power Etiquette is the being overwhelmed. Write your goals and purpose. Check them for completion at the end of six months. You will be pleased at the results.

I decided I needed to eat better and reduce my weight. My doctor and I spoke about it but his suggestions were to eat smaller portions. That was too vague for me. I joined Weight Watchers®, which taught me about better eating. The results? I have followed the plan rigidly and gotten my desired results.

14. Exercise

There is nothing that can substitute for good health. Exercise helps your body function well and makes you feel more alert and able to cope with work challenges. This has been one of the most difficult activities to put into my life. It has come and gone with the decades.

I do not like to exercise regularly at a gym. Recently, I found a way to increase my strength to tone my muscles, which works very well for me. I have a trainer through a program called Super-Slow® (SuperSlow.com). Twenty minutes once a week is "doable" for my lifestyle. The results are phenomenal. I have a stronger body, better posture, and feel healthier. Try some exercise and you will get results as long as you set short-term, reachable goals.

15. Hit the road

Travel opens the mind and helps us appreciate what we have. You may travel on weekends to local celebrations and events or plan annual or semi-annual trips to other countries. There is no doubt that traveling expands your interests and helps you to understand other ways to solve problems. For me, annual European bicycling trips expand my thinking, knowledge, and experience plus provide exercise.

16. Laugh a little

Develop a sense of humor to relieve the stress. It is always better to laugh at yourself and your mistakes. Never play tricks or tell jokes about others, especially co-workers and colleagues.

17. Smile

Smile often, even when you don't feel like it. Smiles are contagious and a smile relieves tension to make people feel more comfortable.

Illustration 1

Magnetic leadership is more than directing people to be more productive; it is about modeling behavior that is thoughtful, creative, sincere, credible, competent and respectful. A leader provides a comfortable, caring environment in which others can express their concerns. When colleagues and co-workers feel valued and respected, they are more productive. The trickle down process works in even the shortest professional ladder. When the leader is thoughtful of others and values their expertise, they are, in turn, caring about those they work with.

Polish the three "V's" for success; then challenge yourself to the power tips that polish your professional leadership skills. Leadership is a continual growth line. As we face new situations, we can weather them. We just need to have a foundation of respectful attitude toward others and ourselves. From there, we must keep learning and improving ourselves because through the process we become better people to lead

Illustration 2

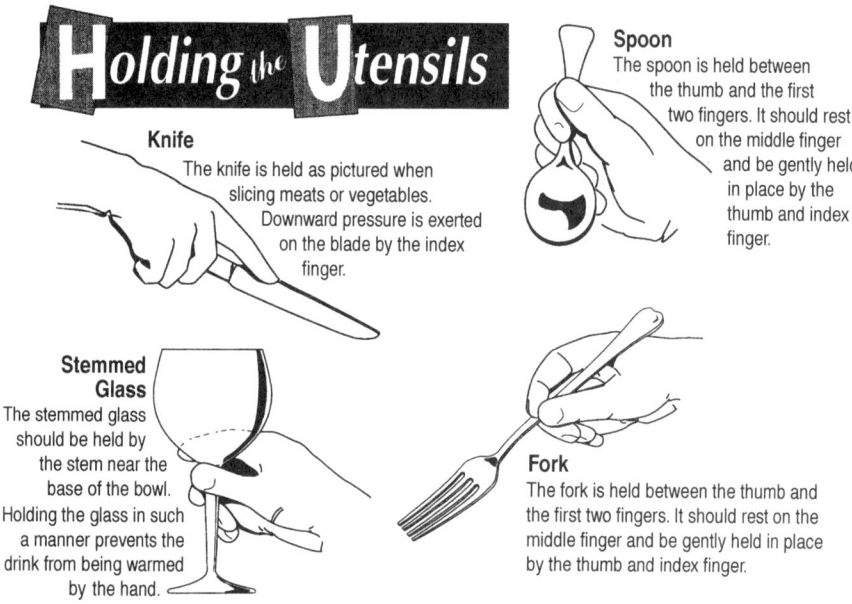

organizations and businesses. The magnetic field is created from the mix of talent and professional presence. You are a leader wherever you go.

Fill your professional package with interesting conversation, an expanse of knowledge, and then wrap it in a pleasing way. Your power comes from being fascinating, honest, highly ethical and caring. Continue to learn and modify your thinking because Power Etiquette is the leadership skills that open doors that money cannot.

About Dana May Casperson

*D*ana May Casperson is the director of The Power Etiquette Group, a company which provides corporations, associations and clients with their ticket to professional success. She helps clients develop their business savvy for enhancing professional and client relationships. Dana May's audiences of all sizes have benefited from her expertise on "Seal the Deal at the Meal," "Moose on the Loose," "Threads of Success," "E-Talk: The New Rules, Power Protocol" and "The Art of Doing International Business." Dana May is an active member of National Speakers Association, California Society of Association Executives, her local Chamber of Commerce and Convention & Visitors Bureau, and is past president of the Sacramento chapter of the National Speakers Association, She is a nationally recognized Power Etiquette Expert who has delivered practical messages for Pacific Bell, the Ritz Carlton Hotels, the Fairmont Hotels, Edward Jones Financial, Allmerica Financial, Medtronics, Sola Optical USA, several universities and business associations.

Contact Information:
Dana May Casperson
The Power Etiquette Group
P.O. Box 3637
Santa Rosa, CA 95402
E-mail: danamay@PowerEtiquette.com
Website: www.PowerEtiquette.com

IF THE LIGHTS ARE OUT, WRITE BY CANDLELIGHT

by Sharon Spano

*L*eaders create extraordinary results based on no evidence that it can be done. It's not easy to accept that leadership is about results. We'd like to think that "some people have it, some people don't." They're just natural born leaders, magnetic, because, well, they just are. That's all there is to it. People are just drawn to them.

But what if part of the reason people are drawn to them is that they're the kind of people who make things happen? It would follow, therefore, that anyone has the potential for leadership because we all have the potential to create results.

What gets in the way, then, is our stories: All the negative tapes we play in our heads, all the excuses why we can't get the job done. Some of us have made an entire career out of telling stories as to why we can't have or will never be. And it's usually someone else's fault instead of our own.

For most of us, this is a hard notion to accept because we don't want to believe we're responsible for results. *If I buy into what Sharon is saying, well, then, I just might be accountable for the way my life is working or, more importantly, not working.*

What I'm asking you to consider is that the stories, in and of themselves, are keeping you from creating extraordinary results. If you don't achieve the results, if you're simply walking around saying, "Well, I'd like to do this, *but* . . . or I'd like to have that, *but* . . . or, I'd like to go there, *but* . . . ," the "but" is the first word in the story. The "but" is keeping you in mediocrity, from having what you deserve.

Before we can explore how to get past the habit of negative storytelling, let me share with you a more specific example of how we sabotage results.

The phone rang, and I could tell by the sound of his voice that Louis was a gentle, caring man.

"Someone told me you could help me," he said. "I have a children's book written, almost three-quarters done."

The idea was wonderful. Louis had created a delightful group of characters surrounding an action-like hero, only this hero was in a wheelchair. Louis had been referred to me for several reasons. One, I have a son who is physically challenged, so I have been a strong voice for the disabled. Two, as a professional speaker, I am before large audiences all across North America. Louis wanted my opinion on the viability of the work. Would it sell? Would kids with disabilities appreciate his main character?

I met with Louis the following afternoon to review his concept of the book and immediately knew that, yes, this was a great idea. My mind raced with possibilities. I imagined Barney-style stuffed toys, t-shirts, maybe even a cartoon flowing from his original concept. For almost two hours, we explored creative possibilities that might come about as a result of the publication of his book. I encouraged him to contact several publishing houses, Disney, and, if all else failed, to consider self-publishing. His project, I believed, was worth whatever effort it would take to create the result: a book that would delight and inspire children with disabilities. Louis left my office exhilarated with a newfound vision for success.

A day after our original meeting, I received a phone call from him asking if I'd consider greater involvement in the project. He felt that I offered a solid business perspective and that my visibility across North America would help generate sales of the book.

"I'm really an artist," he shared. "I don't have much business sense. I'd love for us to be partners on this project. You have the vision for marketing and sales that I don't have."

After several meetings during which we clarified our roles in the project, set forth a sales and marketing plan, and met with an intellectual property attorney, Louis and I agreed that we would enter into a partnership.

Now here's where "his story" starts to unfold, and if I hadn't been so swept up by his creative genius, I might have caught it earlier. You see, Louis had intermittently shared with me some of the challenges he'd been facing. He and his wife were undergoing some financial problems. He had lost his job with a state agency several years earlier due to a whistle-blowing incident he'd been involved in, and, for reasons I never fully understood, he was still unemployed. His wife had also undergone years of manic depression so she, too, was unable to work. Things had been tough for them over the past several years, and Louis really had no money to contribute to the project.

Not a problem, I thought at the time. We've all had times of challenge in our lives. Louis assured me that he was pursuing several job opportunities and that he would have no problem moving forward on the drawings and completion of the book. I was inspired by his openness and assured him that we could build something into the budget that would offset some expenses and help him get back on his feet during the time he was completing the book. What I failed to realize was that Louis had made a career out of engaging in stories that kept him from results. I would soon find out that he had a history of sabotaging his own success.

As we moved more diligently into the process of incorporation, we agreed that Louis must finish his drawings and the rest of the book before I could reasonably approach possible investors. We reviewed our draft of the marketing plan, set timelines, and decided that he would develop a simple storyboard that I could present to interested parties. I began informal discussions with several of my contacts and felt certain that, once they saw his concept and the magnificent drawings, we'd be on our way. Everyone I approached expressed keen interest in the effort and a willingness to invest. Things were moving along nicely. Louis said he could have the storyboard put together in a matter of a week or so. After all, the majority of the drawings were already completed.

Several weeks went by and still no drawings. All the while, Louis and I were having regular conversations about my commitments and progress, but every time I asked him how his drawings were coming, I got, you guessed it, a story.

I've been tired ... sick ... my wife fell ... electricity is out ... and on and on and on it goes until one day, I finally had the courage to address the issue.

"Louis, help me understand," I said, "why it's taking so long to put the board together. The drawings are done. You told me you'd have it in a week or so. Please, tell me what's wrong."

And then, in a fit of rage and blame, Louis lashed out.

"You told me you were going to help me and my wife. You told me you were going to find me money, that you'd get me investors for this project," he screamed.

"I have no money, my lights are out, and I can't pay the bill ... you told me you'd get me money so I could live."

"Louis," I replied. "Yes, I told you I'd find investors for the book, but I'm not responsible for your light bill, your life. I can find investors, but I have to have something to show them, book proposal, drawings, something. I can't ask people to invest in something they've never seen."

The conversation went on at great length, and no matter how hard I tried to get Louis to understand that he must honor his commitment and create the promised result, it always came back to one thing: I was responsible for his life. In essence, he could not write or complete the drawings because I would not pay his light bill.

I probably don't need to tell you that shortly after this conversation, I called a meeting with Louis and explained that we needed to end our relationship. I had already paid the attorney a substantial sum of money and felt it was best to cut the losses before we involved any investors.

This may sound like a harsh, impulsive decision, but what I came to realize about Louis was that he didn't understand *results*. He didn't understand that effective leaders know how to get the job done, no matter what circumstances hit them sideways and knock them over. Another storm? They just swim faster. If the lights are out, they write by candlelight. They understand that if they remain focused on the result, the circumstances take care of themselves.

My experience of Louis in his fit of rage was that he was expecting me to create the results *for* him. I was to find the money, the investors, pay for the attorney, sell the books, and, yes, he was the creative genius, but if the genius refuses to create? If Louis couldn't even create a storyboard, how could I count on him to finish the book? How could I jeopardize my own credibility by asking investors to support a project I now doubted he could finish? How could I, in good conscience, responsibly risk investor dollars?

Louis gave me no choice but to cut my losses and remove myself from the project before it was too late. It pained me greatly to have to look him in the eye and say, "Louis, I'm afraid we have a disparity in our work ethics. You see, I believe that if I focus on the result, I can create that which I desire, even if all the evidence before me says impossible. I live in the probability of 'yes, it can be done.' On the other hand, you live in a conversation that life is against you, and that conversation, is, in effect, sabotaging your success, keeping you from realizing greater results."

As I spoke these words, the greater pain came in knowing that Louis was not yet at a place where he could hear what I was saying or receive it in the spirit in which I was saying it. I felt certain that he would most likely walk away with little understanding of the lesson to be learned. At some level of thought, the story would prevail. Louis would see himself as a victim of circumstances once again. I wanted so badly for him to come to the realization that people rarely want to hear why you *can't* do something. They only care that you *can*. It's always about the results you create, and whether we like it or not, we are judged on those results and how we go about creating them. It's never about the ends justifying the means. It's about moving forward with integrity and doing the right thing, and when you do, everyone involved experiences the outcome as a magnificent effort that has served the greater good. That's essentially what leadership is.

Effective leaders are grounded in integrity and are able to achieve extraordinary results based on no evidence that they can be accomplished. When results are achieved, everybody wins.

Let's talk a bit more specifically about what leaders are like.

First, leaders possess an *Attitude of Abundance*. That's right. Effective leaders know that they deserve abundant results in all they do. They deserve success. It is this belief that gives them the energy to move forward. Consequently, they don't engage in self-negating stories that keep them from achieving results. An Attitude of Abundance takes practice and discipline.

I would venture to guess that Louis had been living in scarcity so long, he began to think that was all he deserved. It was difficult to imagine, even for a moment, that his dream of bringing the book to fruition could come true, so he set about gathering evidence to support this conversation of scarcity. He began to self-sabotage.

Second, effective leaders have *Clarity of Purpose*. They know exactly what they intend to accomplish. That intention is clearly formulated in their thinking and is most often expressed in a written statement. They might even share this commitment with others so as to build a level of accountability. Once the commitment is defined, effective leaders set about engaging in a plan of action as to how they might best achieve their goal. This Clarity of Purpose generates passion, and that passion becomes the driving force that will enable them to overcome any and all obstacles. The voice of passion says, *if the lights are out, write by candlelight.*

Third, effective leaders have the *Confidence to Get The Job Done*. In developing Clarity of Purpose, they discern whether they have the skills and competency to succeed. If, in that process of discernment, they discover they are lacking in any area, they are willing to learn or do what's necessary to bring themselves to the level of required competency. If I'm willing to do what it takes to get the job done, I *will* ultimately experience the result. The combination of competency melded with result equals confidence.

Fourth, effective leaders know how to *Live in the Moment*. They understand the difference between committed action and honest negotiation. They honor their word — no matter what. They do what they say they're going to do. They are reasonable in how they pursue that commitment. They have developed within themselves the ability to discern what is the true priority, and if, in the moment, something more pressing enters the horizon, they are able, from the standpoint of honesty and integrity, to renegotiate the timelines.

You know exactly what I mean. We're not talking about procrastination here. We're talking about the attitude behind the thoughts of, *Go on. Just call and cancel. You can always do it tomorrow.* That's a very different voice from the one that comes from a discerning mind: *Well, I've had an unexpected turn of events today. Let's see what must be addressed. Can this other commitment wait until tomorrow?* When tomorrow comes, the original commitment is the number one priority.

The difference between the two is that one is a choice that comes out of the process of discernment and integrity. The other is a lie, to yourself and the people around you. You know it, and guess what? So does everyone else.

Can you imagine that I might have had a very different response to Louis if he had more expressly told me that he had to focus on getting a job before we could pursue the book project any further? In a process of honest negotiation, he might have told me that his challenges had increased and he needed a few weeks, maybe longer, away from the project until he could regroup. Instead, I got an excuse, a story, each and every day for why he wasn't performing. The pattern of procrastination and story-telling became very evident after just a few short weeks, and it was precisely this pattern that caused me to question his ability to create results.

Going back to our brief discussion of integrity, effective leaders are *trustworthy* in their ability to create results. They have a high level of competency and benevolence. What this essentially means is that they have the skills to get the job done, and they are people who live from principles and a foundation of truth. They have the ability to influence people around them with greater ease. They can enroll others in their vision for success and in doing so create meaningful results with the help of those around them.

Finally, effective leaders are resilient in their pursuit of results because they understand the concept of *Breakdown-Breakthrough*. They realize that sometimes events aren't going to work out as planned. Obstacles get in the way. The action plan is thwarted by circumstances out of our control. In Louis's case, there were many obstacles: Unemployment, lack of resources, a wife who was ill; these are moments of breakdown, obstacles, if you will, that must be taken seriously. Unfortunately, Louis let these breakdowns paralyze him. He engaged in a process of thought that caused him to feel like a victim, and once we fall into the victim trap, as in "why is this happening to me," we are unable to move to a perspective of leadership that allows us to experience the breakthrough.

Here's how that thought process generally works. The breakthrough conversation might sound something like this: *Well, I'm not certain why all of this is happening to me, but let me focus on the result I'm after and figure out where to go from here. What's the lesson I need to learn to move me forward?* The breakthrough may not even appear evident at this point in time, but the effective leader understands that in the midst of chaos, there is order, some greater lesson to be learned.

What are the rewards of being able to create results based on no evidence that they can be accomplished? If you are someone who can make things happen, you will enjoy enhanced credibility, higher self-esteem, and ultimately, you'll find yourself standing before the golden door of opportunity. Every time you venture through that door and create yet another result, you become stronger, more focused, and more passionate about the work you do and the life you live.

So, the question then becomes for each and every one of us, Am I going to settle for mediocrity and continue to make excuses for why my life isn't working or am I going to create results? If the lights are out, am I willing to write by candlelight to do whatever it takes to honor my commitment?

Whether we like it or not, we are judged on results. If you want to know how you're doing, just look to your results. If the results are there, you're probably on the right track. If, on the other hand, you haven't accomplished what you set out to do, you might consider alternative actions. In the end, it's always about results. Everything else is conversation.

About Sharon Spano

Sharon Spano is a speaker and seminar leader on leadership, integrity in the workplace, conflict and confrontation, and life balance and stress. She has a unique way of making every participant feel as though she is speaking directly to them. As one participant said, "Her passionate commitment to her clients and their success is compelling." Sharon's seminars and developmental processes are designed to help companies re-establish a corporate culture where continuous improvement, higher levels of achievement, standards of excellence, and increased customer satisfaction are the norm rather than the exception. She is the author of the international bestselling interactive CD series, How to Handle Conflict and Confrontation. *Corporate leaders agree that Sharon's series,* Principled Leadership: Integrity in the Workplace *is "an incredible opportunity that is motivating, inspirational, and of great value ... with a core message that positively affects the way we do business."*

Contact Information:
Sharon Spano
Spano & Company, Inc.
649 Stonefield Loop
Heathrow, Florida 32746
Phone: (407) 333-0224
Fax: (407) 444-3840
E-mail: Sharon@SharonSpano.com
Website: www.sharonspano.com

SUPER VISION LEADERSHIP

by Jim Lane

Our loud two-bladed choppers beat the air and could be heard for miles. Our goal was to attract the enemy's attention and draw fire. Some called us sitting ducks. The Huey Guns usually went in forty-five minutes to an hour before anyone else. We flew at two to four hundred feet high. When they fired on us, we arrived at a new goal, to overcome the enemy with superior fire power. After the Huey Guns cleared the way, Bird Dog took over. Bird Dog was the call signal for a Cessna 150, a small, two-seat, single-propeller plane that coordinated the large missions.

On my first mission, August 19, 1968, we set out to put 2,500 Marines in the DMZ, the de-militarized zone. The DMZ was the dividing line between North and South Vietnam. The Huey helicopters, the one I flew in, rarely carried passengers unless they were stripped of all armament. The striped version is called a slick. As a gun ship, it had a seven-shot rocket pod and two M-60 machine guns mounted on each side for the pilot to shoot. The large side doors behind the pilot and co-pilot were removed. M-60 machine guns were mounted in the door openings. The crew chief sat on the left and the door gunner on the right behind the pilot. Huey's flew in pairs, lead and chase. The choppers that carry fifteen combat-ready "grunts" had a five-man crew. Grunt is the nickname for Combat Infantry. The transport choppers flew in threes.

I was in the second of a pair of Huey Guns. We were up at a thousand feet watching the air show and waiting for our turn in the action, knowing it was coming soon. The grunt transport choppers flew just above the tree tops. By the time you could hear them, they were out of sight. The first three choppers landed a hundred feet south of the Ben Hai River, in the center of the DMZ, and let out fifteen men each. The men quickly disappeared into the jungle. The lead chopper disappeared in an explosion after taking a direct hit from heavy artillery. A second explosion hit the river bank. The Ben Hai River, the center of the DMZ, flows into the Black Sea at the seventeenth parallel. The second chopper, now in front, took some shrapnel. The crew ran into the woods. The third chopper took off immediately. A second volley of two artillery rounds came in from the north. This time they were off target. The crew that had run into the woods, with the grunts, decided to go back to their helicopter and leave.

Bird Dog called for more air support. Two F4 Phantom jets, carrying eighteen, 500-pound bombs each, appeared. They were on target in a heartbeat. When the jets left, it looked like a thriving ant hill on the north side of the river. The enemy, said Bird Dog, had at least 45 men looking to get in on the action. The first two gun ships threw in all they had and went back to base for more ammo. It was our turn. We rolled in hot. Every time the pilot pointed our chopper toward the enemy, he would give the command, "Make me hot." For safety, the rockets and machine guns he controlled could not be fired unless they were switched on at the control panel. The co-pilot hit the switches. The pilot threw in rockets and nailed the "hippies," as we called them, with his four M-60s all the way down. When he turned, I had the advantage and kept shooting until we were out of range. We continued rolling in hot until we exhausted our ammo. We went to LZ Stud, a close landing pad, for a hot rearming and refueling and returned for more action. Hot rearm and refuel mean you do not shut the engine down so you can get right back to the action.

Days earlier, they had taken me up and put me through the gauntlet. My most practical training came at a thousand feet as I watched the other crews. My heart throbbed in my throat as I wondered what would happen when it was my turn. All fears were forgotten when my machine gun sounded off.

August 19, 1968, my first day of action, was a long one. We took off after breakfast. We stayed on target but did not put in any more men. We gave cover for our forty five grunts on the ground. When we returned to base that evening, I went to the chow hall. My gut wrenched.

I thought of the five men who ate breakfast here this morning but did not come back. I kept seeing their chopper disappear in an explosion.

Days later I was given Air Crewman Combat Wings. The main requirement for these wings was three strike missions. A strike mission requires enemy fire. I had four strike missions that day. When I came aboard, they told me it usually takes two months to get wings and many never get them.

After I was out of the Marines for several months, and more than a year after the incident, I received a call from the Marines Headquarters in Key West. I was asked to come and receive a Single Air Medal with a Bronze Star for the First Award for the action I participated in on August 19, 1968. The medal says "for heroic action during aerial flight during combat." At that moment I realized I had instinctively applied the top driving force of leaders; I had clear vision. In the Huey, my vision was crystal clear as to my mission, duties, and responsibilities. This was a long way from what my life had been like before Vietnam.

Four strike missions my first day. As the days went by, the action I saw continued to increase. I ended up with more strike missions and saw more action than all of the men in my shop put together. "Lane's flying! Something's happening!" became the buzz. I flew to the frontlines, where the bullets flew. Looking down the gun barrel of enemy machine guns, I could see the tracer rounds coming. The tracer rounds have phosphorus on the tip of the projectile. The friction removes the coating and it begins to burn so you can see them. When a tracer grows to the size of an orange and moves to the side, it will miss you. If a tracer grows to the size of an orange and does not appear to move, it may have your name on it. I could not see four out of five rounds because only every fifth round was a tracer.

Vision = Run

Recently, I talked with a man who was in the Marines. He was in Vietnam at the same time as I. He then got a good job, retired young, and has his yard looking like he wants. He is now wondering what to do with the rest of his life. Many people live life on the surface. When their life is over, they could say that they followed all the rules but never found any purpose to life. They may provide well for their families, but their zest for life is missing.

A man with a vision for building character into his life and well grounded on principles will never wonder what to do next. He will be running hard, wondering if he can finish before his life is over. Clear vision gives purpose and a reason to keep running.

In war, young men fight on the frontlines. The mature men direct the young men. Maturity is a result of

1. Learning rules
2. Internalizing principles
3. Building character
4. Equipping others

Character training is the judicious application of pressure until the right response is achieved. I learned the rules when they took me up for training. I wrote a letter to my mother explaining the day and told her of the eight hundred rounds I fired in training. I observed the principles at one thousand feet up as I watched the first two choppers hit the enemy. I internalized the principles and built character in the weeks following. Then I began to train others as door gunners. Although you may not be fighting an actual war, real battles take place every day in everyone's life. Are you winning?

So Little . . . So Much . . . Vision, Vision, Vision

As a kid, my vision of the future was almost nonexistent. I did not have any focus. I stumbled out of bed in the morning and mindlessly ate breakfast. My friend Billy would come by my house and walk me to the bus stop. I repeated the first grade. I went to summer school every year in high school. I came back for the first semester of twelfth grade a second time, failed, and decided it was time to give up. I left school humiliated and with no future plans. I was not leadership material. I did not even know how to lead myself.

The only girl I dated in school worked in the principal's office. Confessing one day that she had looked through my school records, she thought I should know I had the lowest IQ of any of the fellows she had dated. (That was a lesson in how to not motivate someone!)

My high school year book has my picture with only my name next to it. The high school leaders have their clubs, sports, and accomplishments listed next to their names. As I look back, I wonder how so many with so much do so little and so few with so little do so much? Vision! Vision!

Before going to Vietnam, I was sent to special weapons school. We were trained to load, test, and fuse smart weapons in 1966. There I met a warrant officer, Mr. Moody. I was in the first A6 squadron in the Marines at Cherry Point, North Carolina. Mr. Moody asked me to move to the second A6 squadron to lead the new men coming from ordnance school. Ordnance is anything that explodes. I was stunned he would ask. I said "yes." The most unlikely leader was chosen.

From special weapons, I progressed to nuclear weapons. I am sure it had something to do with handling all that power — power emboldens most men. I enjoyed the class and excelled. The vision of leading the new men in the ordnance shop came from a leader, Mr. Moody. The clearly defined goals came from my instructors at a condensed ordnance school on the Marine base where we handled all the weapons. The new men came from a Navy base. Instead of handling weapons, they had sat in classes for 18 months. I was able to teach guys with more time in the military and of higher rank than I. Being entrusted with the authority to direct men's lives was the most powerful weapon I had ever handled (it still is).

I chose to extend my service in Vietnam rather than return to the States to fight the "spit and polish war" or to face spending what should have been free time picking up cigarette butts. After the extension papers were signed, a new gunny sergeant just in from the States, who had never seen action, decided he would run the war the same way he had learned to control people stateside. When the squadron first sergeant saw me picking up cigarette butts, he told me I did not need to be doing that. Picking up cigarette butts is a form of punishment. He offered me a transfer to a helicopter squadron and I elected to go. My third day in the ordnance shop I was chosen again to lead. This time there was another corporal with three months more time in rank than me. I saw myself as a leader, and I was getting comfortable taking charge. This was a good thing as the other corporal did not want to lead and asked me not to tell anyone about his seniority. He did not see himself as a leader. Too bad for him; a supervisor must have super vision.

During boot camp at Parris Island in 1965, every night just before going to bed we recited that we were willing to die for our country and "the Lord's Prayer." The training took place late in 1965, but the possibility that I might not come back hit me squarely when I got into a Huey gun ship loaded for battle in 1968. Conviction is a belief strong enough to die for, persuasion is a weak belief that may change under pressure. A positive response to a crucible experience is the best preparation for leadership.

Your response reveals your attitude. People looking for someone to follow are watching for your response in difficult times. Do not lose your confidence; it will be richly rewarded.

If you have a vision worthy of living for and valuable enough to die for, you can expect others to follow. Most people are bored with their life style and welcome an invitation to join in a cause. The vision of the leader excels the view of laity. Followers focus on rights, leaders on responsibilities.

Becoming a Man

In the Marines I went from being a boy to being a man. I learned how to be a leader. I learned how to focus on what needs to be done. I learned how to get others to follow my vision based on the steadiness of my convictions.

In 1995 I had an opportunity to impart some of what I had learned to boys at a technical school. That summer I was invited to be a guest lecturer for a week, and I prepared a message for the boys on accepting responsibility and leading roles in life. However, while I was talking, a thought popped into my head. I had always wondered *when does a boy become a man?* I asked them, was it . . .

- At age 12 like Jesus in the Temple?
- At age 13 because now you're a teen?
- At age 16 and old enough to drive a car?

- At age 18 when you become legally responsible before the law and can serve in the military?
- At age 21 surely now that you could vote and drink?
- In boot camp?
- Upon returning from war?
- At the marriage altar?
- After his first baby is born?

The question was rhetorical, but it lingered in my mind. From their faces I sensed they wanted to know an answer, too. So I led them in an assignment. I asked them to tell me the difference between men and boys. They were to think on the subject that evening and answer in class the next day. Their answers varied but several used the key word I was looking for. One said, "I think it is when you turn 50." Most of the guys had good answers and contributed to the lesson. I was looking for one key word, *responsibility*. In the class with me were two young men who were apprenticed to me in my business. One of those young men worked with me to write the following. The process that transforms boys to men are the same that transform ineffective leaders to powerful leaders.

The Difference between Men and Boys

The Timing of Manhood
- When you have exceeded the wisdom of your teachers
- When you learn to recognize and heed warning signals
- When you have been transformed from a taker to a giver
- When you consistently rise early, plan the day, and take control of the circumstances
- When your parents "promote you," mom's apron strings are cut, and you help meet her needs

The Responsibility of Manhood
- Is striving towards excellence
- Is continuing to study and learn all you can
- Is investing in the lives of children to create a legacy to outlast

yourself
- Is structuring your life around that which cannot be destroyed or taken away
- Is discerning purpose in your life and developing character to stay on course

The Character of Manhood
- He is serious-minded and chooses mature friends
- He is guided by universal, non-optional principles of life
- He is committed to a noble plan for his life and submits to authorities
- He is determined to accomplish worthy goals at the right time, regardless of opposition

---

A boy often thinks he is a man. *A man realizes how childish he is.*

A boy tries to be right in everything. *A man knows he is vulnerable and imperfect.*

A boy seeks excitement. *A man is excited with a moment of peace.*

A boy uses his speech to express himself. *A man uses his speech to draw out the thoughts of others, as well.*

A boy is content only when he is fulfilled. *A man is fulfilled just to be content.*

A boy has big dreams and ambitious plans. *A man keeps his big dreams, but makes plans patiently.*

A boy cries when he is hurt. *A man cries when there is a great loss.*

A boy is eager to be known. *A man is eager to know.*

A boy finds happiness in what he is doing. *A man finds joy in who he is being.*

A boy's next week is a long wait away. *A man's next week is suddenly upon him.*

A boy looking into the future sees distant fog. *A man looking into the future sees the importance of decisions today.*

— Copyright 1995, 2001 by Jim C. Lane

Having spent a week with these young men, shaping their vision and defining their goals, I sent each of them a copy of *The Difference Between Men & Boys* with hopes they would review it often, define their goals, and run toward their vision.

America is weak when men are weak. Men are weak when leaders write more rules and laws instead of training men. Children should be told the rules. Men should be trained with the principles. Do not feed a man a fish, teach him how to fish. Teach him how to lead with vision.

Super Vision is Clear and Compelling

A vision is an unfulfilled need. It is not real yet, but you have a clear and compelling conviction that you can make it real. At first all that can be seen are the problems. In the seeking process to find out how the need can be met many questions are asked. Your vision develops as you find the answers.

Super Vision Puts Courage in Others

People cannot see a vision of a good future when a previous failure blocks their view. As a leader, give them some of your courage and help them out of their fog. Only then will they will be able to run with confidence. Many are not willing to deal with their problems, so they end up following the vision of someone already on the run. Every young person is looking for direction. Many will follow anyone who involves them in a mission. They cannot live up to expectations without help and are easily disappointed. After disappointment comes discouragement, especially if encouragement is in short supply (I like to say, "Encouragement happens when someone puts his courage in me."). Disillusionment and despair can follow.

Super Vision Sees the End

The vision is what it looks like at the end. The plan is how to get there. Don't confuse the two. The vision may come into clearer focus but the plan changes often to meet the objectives. A vision always involves helping others. All leaders get nearsighted sometimes, focusing on themselves instead of their vision. When self-centeredness is overcome, the vision comes into focus.

A vision often takes more time to fulfill than originally expected and may be more difficult than imagined. Keep a journal. When you begin to recruit others to help, tell them of the need and value of their getting involved. Explain what you want them to do and ask them to join the vision, not you. Be able to explain the vision in one sentence. Get a commitment to begin working right away to make the vision a reality.

Super Vision Looks for Leaders

Most of my woodworking business involves building stairs. A few years ago we started supplying parts to other stair builders. The parts business has the capacity to outgrow the craftsmanship business. My sons work with me, and I hope to turn the business over to them. I explained to them that we must not give up manufacturing stairs. When we quit building stairs, we lose the cutting edge. My firstborn is 26 and runs the shop. I home school my seventeen and twelve-year-old sons. They go to work with me every day. They spend mornings in the office with their academics and afternoons in the shop. My base of operation is my sons. My speaking outreach is to men. I do not want to lose my cutting edge with men, so I continue working with my boys and work with other young men also.

My old friend Billy doesn't come by anymore, and I don't need coffee in the morning to get a jump start. I used to go to bed early and get up late, now I go to bed late and get up early. After I assumed responsibility for myself, I accepted responsibility for others who lined up behind me. My vision became clear and I worked on practical steps of action. As I mature, the less productive activities are delegated to others so I can focus on helping more people. Leadership is expensive. The price tag is restriction from many pleasures, but the rewards are worth all the sacrifices.

Become a man by going through the process.
Become a leader by recognizing the process and leading others.

A boy is changed by outward conformity. A man is transformed from inward character. A leader is developed with a vision.

The difference between little boys and big boys is the price of their toys. The difference between boys and men is responsibility. Boys make excuses and spend their time playing. Men take responsibility and spend their time turning their vision into a reality. People are looking for responsible leaders with vision. Get rid of the toys and the boys will follow. Give your vision to willing followers. Some will go back to their toys, some will follow your vision, and some will acquire super vision and become responsible leaders.

About Jim Lane

*J*im Lane is president of Character Vision, an organization that teaches people to voice virtue — with a walk that speaks louder than their talk — and leave a legacy for future generations. "History exalts unknown people," he has observed, "whose character made them respond nobly to unexpected challenges that carried them to prominence." Jim teaches managers and leaders how to build enthusiasm in employees for their work through building character, which in turn gives them tools to take home so they can equip their family. He gives people the building blocks for enduring success, which impacts decision making, integrity, and personal effectiveness. He also helps companies find people with character qualities important to the position, which promotes accomplishment and saves money. Jim is a consultant and keynoter, as well as an instructor of NCFCA, an organization that trains home schooled youth 12-18 years old for public speaking and debate. Jim served in the Marines in Vietnam and received several medals, including the Single Mission Air Medal for heroic achievement in aerial combat flight. He is the founder of Jim Lane Craftsman & Stair Parts by Lane, a business being turned over to his three sons.

Contact Information:
Jim Lane
Character Vision
607 South Evers Street
Plant City, FL 33563
Phone: (813) 754-5779
Fax: (813) 759-6631
E-mail: Jim@CharacterVision.net
Website: www.CharacterVision.net

Motivating Others to Do What You Want

by Doug Smart, CSP

Everyone is motivated. That's a fact that will help you, as a leader, bring out the best in others. You can rely on this principle to get virtually anything accomplished. True, a person may not be motivated to do what you want, the way you want it or when you want it (my son comes to mind and the angst he expresses over his chores of emptying the dishwasher and mowing the lawn), but each person holds certain personal "motivators" that appeal to a personal sense of comfort. Comfort, in this case, is not about lounging, laziness or being pampered; it is based on the individual's personality style. Everyone — even teenagers, co-workers and customers — has comfort triggers that cause positive responses (motivators) or negative responses (de-motivators). Recognizing these comfort triggers will make it easier for you to motivate others to do what needs to be done.

Directiveness and Affiliativeness

Spotting and understanding motivators and de-motivators are based on two traits we all share in common, "directness" and "affiliativeness." Let's first look at directiveness.

Some have a strong need to direct what is happening around them. They enjoy telling other people what to do and how to do it, and they are seen as assertive. For example, this could be the person who regularly volunteers to chair committees, frequently voices opinions, and finds decision making exciting.

At the opposite end are people who are comfortable following the lead of others. They take direction well, don't feel it is necessary to stand out in order to be effective, and are uneasy making definitive decisions. They often defer to others.

Actually, when it comes to directiveness, each of us moves up and down a directiveness scale depending upon the events. For example, in a tense moment, such as perceiving that someone might be a threat to your children, your gut reaction could zoom instantly to a super-direct position, causing even the meekest to bark, "Get away from here! Leave my family alone!" You suddenly epitomize the top of the scale. Conversely, there are situations in which you readily become submissive, such as when you are stopped for speeding and you realize you can't avoid the ticket. Your mild-mannered side responds with a decidedly non-assertive, submissive, "Yes, officer."

Through the years you have become comfortable operating out of one of four stages of directiveness: very direct, mildly direct, mildly deferential and very deferential. You live in one of the four stages more than the other three and the people who know you best can identify which of the four is most comfortable for you.

The second trait is our affiliativeness. Some people have a strong need to be around other people. They relate well to the feelings and needs of others and are particularly intuitive about the emotional state of others. They tend to be relationship focused. At the opposite are people who are task focused. They are practical, organized and traditional. They aren't fond of small talk. Given a choice between socializing and completing a task, they prefer to do the task

If you imagine affiliativeness as a horizontal line, you can see that you shift back and forth depending on the circumstances. Sometimes you feel like "the life of the party" and you are on the far left end of the line — the socializing end. Other times you might have people around you and you think (or even say), "I love you dearly but I wish you would shut-up and leave me alone! I have work to do!" That's when you're on the far right end of the line — the task-oriented end.

Habitually, you favor one of four stages of affiliativeness: very social, mildly social, mildly task oriented and very task oriented. You live in one of the four stages more than the other three and here, too, the people who know you well can identify which of the four is a fit for your personality.

The Four Success Styles

Combining these two traits, directiveness and affiliativeness, gives us a personality quadrant. Each of the four success styles has its strengths and weaknesses, and no style is superior to any other. All are necessary ingredients to a vibrant, fully functioning workplace. To make it easy to remember them, I've given color names to the four styles.

Direct + social = orange
Direct + task = red
Deferential + task = purple
Deferential + social = blue

Take a look at the Strengths Chart. As you read, you'll see yourself in every corner. As a complex human being juggling vastly different responsibilities, you tap into your talents in each of the success styles. However, through the years you have come to favor one style more than the other three, and that's reflected in your personality. You are more comfortable operating out of one corner more than the others. A strength that's developed to an extreme runs the risk of being interpreted by others as a weakness. The Weaknesses Chart is another tool for determining the corner from which a person habitually operates.

In my workshops, the class participates in an exercise that matches well-known American personalities with the colors. The majority opinion is that President Bill Clinton is Orange, Senator Hillary Clinton is Red, President George W. Bush is Purple, and President Ronald Reagan is Blue. Besides serving as a fun practice in spotting personality styles, it's a useful way to demonstrate that a person can be any of the four success styles and be president of the United States (or close to it).

Each of the four success styles enjoys comfort triggers (motivators) that feed their needs. The oranges are particularly comforted (motivated) by attention paid to them — they enjoy being noticed and appreciated. The reds are comforted by a sense of control over a situation or task. The purples are comforted by a sense of accuracy — they relish the sensation that things are working out as they are supposed to. And the

STRENGTHS
assertive

	Orange	*Red*	
	persuasive	decisive	
	spontaneous	strong-willed	
	dramatic	high achiever	
	outgoing	very direct	
	pursues change	organized	
	talkative	traditional	
	adventurous	competitive	
	dreamer	likes control	
	opinionated	goal-oriented	

Affiliative
social-oriented ··· **task-oriented**

	Blue	*Purple*	
	loyal	practical	
	friendly	thorough	
	caring	factual	
	loving	reserved	
	gregarious	persistent	
	good listener	meticulous	
	informal	task-focused	
	agreeable	has high standards	
	calm	risk avoider	

Directive
deferential

blues are comforted by a sense of closeness — they especially value situations in which care for others (including themselves) is an important element.

There are also discomfort triggers that these serve as de-motivators. A leader who de-motivates someone, even unwittingly, will have a difficult time gaining that person's co-operation in doing what needs to be done. Here are some examples: The oranges feel uncomfortable when kept waiting. Actually, I think most people dislike waiting, but an orange tends to perceive being kept waiting as a sign that he is not special, and he may become defensive or argumentative to draw atten-

WEAKNESSES
assertive

Orange	***Red***
pushy	stubborn
overbearing	dominates
manipulative	closed
disorganized	critical
undisciplined about time	expects immediate results
restless	unapproachable
exaggerates	Iinsensitive
Blue	***Purple***
too other-oriented	slow
indecisive	perfectionistic
vulnerable	extra-cautious
impractical	dislikes surprises
dislikes change	withdrawn
	passive

Affiliative / *Directive*

deferential

tion to his needs. The reds are particularly uncomfortable with exaggerated, mushy emotional displays.

Lavish praise, for instance, may be interpreted as inappropriate and insincere. The purples have little patience for carelessness and sloppiness.

The "YOU CAN DO IT!" just "fake it 'til you make it" attitude of some oranges will be a turn-off. The blues are uncomfortable with insensitive people. A leader who tends to focus on the "bottomline" to the detriment of other people's feelings will lose the confidence and loyalty of a blue.

Applying Motivators and Avoiding De-Motivators

Is it important for leaders to recognize and respond to different people's emotional needs? Of course it is. What if, for example, you are an orange (motivated by attention) and your employee is a purple (motivated by accuracy) and you're in the habit of dropping bombs on your

Motivators

Orange	*Red*
attention	control
recognition	mastery
achievement	loyalty
excitement	responsibility
adventure	fast pace
spontaneity	

Blue	*Purple*
affirmation	accuracy
kindness	practical
popularity	information
closeness	autonomy
caring	consistency
	perfection

employee like this: "Look, don't put a lot of effort into it, but I need you to give me a rough estimate on the projected sales for the next three years if we merge with the Lopez Company. Also run the numbers on opening either a Mexico City or Santiago office, but without the merger. I need it in an hour so I can make a report at the meeting. I forgot to ask you to do this after last week's meeting. Sorry. Just do the best you can." A purple will likely tense like a deer frozen in the headlights and mutter that you are impossible to work with. She may agree to see what she can do, but even if she gives you numbers by the deadline, don't expect her to feel proud of her work, and do expect resentment toward your loose style. Here's some sample dialog that could better meet her needs while getting the best job possible: "I forgot to ask you for something I need for the meeting in an hour. Please prepare a best-guess estimate for three years of projected sales if we merge with Lopez. Also, give me an idea of what the numbers would be if we don't merge but instead open either a Mexico City or Santiago office. We discussed this at the last two managers' meetings. I have the minutes; these will help you. I apologize

DE-MOTIVATORS

Orange	*Red*
lack of enthusiasm	time wasters
wanting	irreverence
indecision	laziness
conventional thinking	emotional display
Blue	***Purple***
insensitivity	over-assertiveness
argument	carelessness
insincerity	arrogance
self-centeredness	fakes

for asking at the last minute. I won't hold you to your estimates. However I need general numbers now and we can refine them later. How reliable will the data be? What resources do you need now to get this done? When can I have accurate numbers? Thank you."

Here are some other combinations to consider. What if a red continuously barked orders at a blue without regard for the latter's feelings? What if a blue spent an hour gushing to a red about the wonderful opportunities for strengthening relationships that a new project will afford? Consider how an orange would feel in a job with a purple boss who was "all work and no play." The Bible says, "Do unto others as you would have them do unto you." However, different people have different comfort triggers. One style of communicating information is not equally effective among the four success styles. How can you apply knowledge of people's different comfort and discomfort triggers to motivate people to do what you know needs to be done? Here are some suggestions.

Putting Knowledge into Action

Take a look at the people you work with the most. Do you see that some individuals have a high need to direct while others are content in a highly deferential role? Do you see that some individuals are highly social in their temperament while others are much more task oriented?

Blue

Do:
- Socialize
- Be open, honest, vulnerable
- Demonstrate trust and need
- Show that you care
- Ask "how" questions to generate discussion
- Show appreciation for contributions
- Choose casual over formal
- Be sensitive to feelings in disagreements

Don't:
- Talk 100% business
- Be afraid to discuss feelings
- Expect immediate decisions
- Threaten or dominate to prompt responses
- Favor facts and figures over people issues
- Patronize

Purple

Do:
- Be analytical in your approach
- Liberally use facts, figures, and substantiation
- Be direct and specific
- Be realistic
- Focus on the task
- Outline action steps
- Provide evidence — and allow him/her to verify your information

Don't:
- Spontaneously discuss important issues
- Try to rush the decision-making process
- Make changes "off the cuff"
- Whine or try to manipulate
- Be disorganized in your presentation
- Interpret "no response" as approval

Recognizing that different people have different comfort triggers that motivate or de-motivate them will help you meet their needs and bring forth their best behaviors and attitudes. There's no limit to what your leadership can accomplish if other people are motivated to do what you know needs to be done.

About Doug Smart, CSP

*I*n 1998 the National Speakers Association awarded Doug Smart their highest certification, Certified Speaking Professional. Doug is a writer, publisher and radio show host of "Smarter by the Minute" and "The Millionaire Show." He has spoken at over 1,000 conventions, conferences, seminars, sales rallies and management retreats around the world. Doug is author and co-author of Thriving in the Midst of Change, TimeSmart: How Real People Really Get Things Done at Work, Wholehearted Success, Fantastic Customer Service Inside & Out, *and* Irresistible Leadership.

Contact Doug's office for an information kit on bringing The Get Smart Series to your organization.

Contact Information:
Doug Smart
Smart Business Seminars
P.O. Box 768024
Roswell, GA 30076
Phone: (770) 587-9784
E-mail: Doug@DougSmart.com
Website: www.DougSmart.com

True Leaders Lead Themselves First

By Dr. Bill Newman

I learned a lesson from an unconscious, false, and limiting belief that nearly cost me my life twice in one day. I was on a marlin fishing vacation with my friend, Jim, in Baja California Sur, Mexico. The fishing was so good we decided that we had caught enough marlin and wanted to experience another adventure. We had heard of a beautiful waterfall that periodically flowed in the mountains high above the desert. A long hike across the desert and deep into the mountains to discover a beautiful oasis was the adventure we were looking for.

To avoid overexposure to the scorching sun, we started early in the morning. After some effort, we discovered the trail entrance near a small ranch and a dried riverbed. Two barking ranch dogs startled us, but some pleasant words and pats on their heads made them friendly towards us and they followed for quite a way, eventually running and barking far ahead of us.

Although it was January and despite an early morning start, the dry heat of the desert sun drew the moisture from our bodies as rapidly as we could replenish it from our limited water supply. To avoid the sharp thorns of the brush and the needles of the cacti, we steadily picked our way along the dried riverbed.

Suddenly, the dogs' barking exploded in the stifling air. Its pitch and frequency rose urgently, as if to say, "Come quickly! We need your help! Now!" Approaching the excited dogs, we were alarmed to see the muscle and bone exposed in the shoulder of one bleeding dog and the dangling ear and jawbone of the other. My heart pounded furiously as I quickly scanned this no-man's-land for the creature that had inflicted those ugly wounds. I felt we were prey! As we approached the dogs, we were astonished that they courageously leapt as fast as their broken bodies could carry them *towards* their enemies. It was as if they were protecting us from the same savage attack they had suffered. Their sacrifice spared us.

Although the savage attack of the dogs left us shaken, we tenaciously continued onward to find a waterfall in the mountains of a desert. The ever-narrowing, dry riverbed led us up and along steep, rocky cliffs. Nearly exhausted, we finally came to the top of a high vertical ledge, the stone shelf from which the water fell. We imagined how beautiful it would be if only there was water. It was much to dry for the river to be flowing at this time of year. Far below the cliff we could see a pool of water that had not yet dried up. From such a distance, we could not determine the depth of the water. We decided to climb down to find out, which meant taking a risk by traversing a narrow crack in the high, vertical cliff above the pool.

Ahead of me, Jim, either less patient or more eager than I and about half way across the narrow rock ledge of the mountain, got in trouble. I watched a surreal scene as he took just a few steps on the steepest part of the crack in the rock wall and heard him scream, "Oh no!" I watched him fall down the cliff wall.

Jim survived the near death fall, but soon thereafter encountered his second near death experience. We were attacked by the black creatures upon our descent of the mountain. When they ferociously attacked us, I saw Jim quickly turn and run for his life, with a look of horror on his ghost-white face. Simultaneously, I saw the black creature, with long razor-ike tusks, blast out of the cave like a heat-seeking missile. With blazing speed, it was gaining rapidly on Jim. Then, Jim tripped in the hot, deep sand of the desert floor. At that instant, the image of dragging his bloody, dead body through the desert flashed through my mind. I helplessly watched the wild boar pounce. Jim lay there helplessly, with his head cocked around to see the ferocious boar upon him. Suddenly our friends came out of nowhere! The boar fled with the dogs close behind.

As I helped Jim up from his devastating ordeal, I thought how relieved I felt that he had escaped two near-death experiences in the same day. He was still in a state of shock and did not say much. We agreed it was time to return to our origination point as soon as possible. We were exhausted, traumatized, and severely dehydrated. Jim drank from his canteen. I yearned for a sip, which I did not request. I had depleted my water supply long ago on the mountain top. My mouth and throat were parched and my energy was rapidly declining.

After walking about two hours, we stopped to determine on what path to continue. There were several paths leading south, the direction from which we had we started. However, none of them looked familiar. We estimated that we had hiked for about seven hours. Since we had climbed uphill and stopped with the dogs for battles, we were hopeful we could make better time going back.

While Jim was suffering primary trauma, I was suffering secondary trauma from witnessing his two horrific experiences. I was unconscious of how my traumatized state would affect my response to the peril that we would encounter next. Jim still had water and I was desperately desiring water in a way I had never imagined I could. I felt such urgency to return to our truck for water. Unfortunately, we couldn't agree and chose different paths, journeying on alone. I walked slowly in the scorching sun for hours. My energy was steadily waning until there was none. I was severely dehydrated, depleted of energy, and lost. I just kept taking small steps in the direction that felt right. I would walk a short distance, stop, lie down to rest, and get up again to start over. Each time I got up, it was harder to stand. The distances between my rests became shorter as my rests became longer. I kept fighting off a recurring thought each time my steps grew weaker. Finally, I couldn't get up. I couldn't swallow, feel my lips, my mouth, or my tongue. Prostrate, on the hot sand, in the scorching desert sun, too weak to get up again, it happened. The thought came back and I could not stop it this time: "I am going to die." And then other thoughts followed. "What is it going to be like to die this way? Why am I dying this way? Will I ever be found in this wilderness? I never expected to die this way." Then my rapid stream of thoughts stopped and a feeling of serenity came over me as I sat up and looked out over the desert, squinting, with the bright, hot sun in my eyes. A new thought broke into my consciousness: "I will survive!"

Then I stood up again and began walking in the direction of the dried riverbed. I kept thinking *if I can find the riverbed and follow it, it will lead me back to the truck.* I walked with renewed conviction, in small steps, fueled by the determination and passion to live!

Suddenly, in the distance I could hear squealing and then growling sounds. As I walked in small steps, the sounds became louder and louder. I knelt down on one knee to peer below the thick brush and thorny trees. At first I thought I was hallucinating. The squeals and growls were now joined by a chorus of hoof beats. When I was low enough to see what I heard, I knew it was real! It was them! A whole herd of bristling, black creatures with razor sharp tusks racing straight towards me.

I jumped to my feet and ran as fast as I could to the nearest tree. I pulled my weak body up its thorny trunk and branches in what seemed like slow motion. As I watched my attackers running around and jumping up the tree, I was clinging to it for dear life, blood streaming from my arms, legs, stomach and chest. My body was punctured and sliced by the long, sharp thorns of the same tree that was sustaining my life for that moment. I shouted as loud as I could with my parched mouth and throat: "Jim! Jim!"

I was not heard by Jim, but I was not unheard. It happened again! Out of nowhere the dogs appeared! As the sound of their barks grew closer and closer, it became like the sound of music to me announcing the arrival of my saviors. When the dynamic duo approached the tree, my aggressors scattered.

I did not wait a second longer than their departure to descend the tree and continue my journey. Having survived this attack, I had no doubt I would live. With renewed vitality, I slowly dragged my bloody body towards the riverbed. By that time, I could hear Jim's voice shouting my name in the distance. I returned his call and then waited for his arrival. Jim then walked ahead to find the riverbed and returned to help me walk back to our truck with him.

Both Jim and I had two near-death experiences that day. I was more afraid of dying by dehydration than I was of being shredded by the tusks of the desert devils. They were either wild boars or javelinas or both. Wild boars have curved tusks and javelinas have straight tusks. We saw both on that day from hell.

My two near-death experiences taught me that *what I do not know can kill me*. That is, what I believe unconsciously may affect my choices for actions that could lead to death. I made a decision to part from Jim at a point in our journey that drastically decreased our odds of survival. I was right about the most direct route to our destination and wrong about the most effective way to get there.

I rejected Jim's suggestion to stay together on our hike because I knew the right direction, which he declined to follow. I had an unconscious, false, and limiting belief that I could not trust others with something as important as my life or survival. This unconscious belief had grown out of my past experiences with betrayal. Now that I am conscious of this past unconscious belief, I can make new choices in this domain that are win/win, both personally and professionally.

You, too, can overcome the obstacles of your leadership mindset to become a highly effective and true leader. First: by identifying and changing your unconscious, false, and limiting beliefs about yourself that cause your negative or low self-concept, also known as your self-image. Beliefs about yourself, internally, pertain to your self-worth, self-confidence, self-efficacy, and self-acceptance. Second, you overcome mindset obstacles by identifying and changing your unconscious, false, and limiting beliefs about your life experiences that negatively affect your choices and behavior. Beliefs about your life experiences, externally, refer to your interpretations of the meaning of your life encounters. Hereafter, I will describe your false and limiting beliefs as simply "negative beliefs" and refer to your self-concept as your "self-image."

As your first obstacle, your low self-image causes your low self-esteem. You become a highly effective and true leader when first, you lead yourself with high self-esteem. High self-esteem manifests itself when you develop a habit of self-acceptance. Your self-esteem is what you experience as a result of your choice and action of self-acceptance.

Without your choice to take action for self-acceptance, you will not have the experience of self-esteem.

You overcome your first obstacle of your mindset by developing high self-esteem through your habit of self-acceptance. There are three aspects of self-acceptance. They are: 1. Your self-value. 2. Your willingness to experience. 3. Your compassion for yourself.

The first aspect of self-acceptance is a fundamental orientation of self-value and self-commitment that derives from the fact that I am alive and conscious; it is more primitive than self-esteem. It is an act of self-affirmation, a kind of natural egoism that is the birthright of every human being. Yet we have the power to act against and nullify it.

An attitude of self-acceptance can inspire an individual to face whatever he or she needs to encounter without self-hatred, repudiating one's value, or relinquishing the will to live. It embraces the declaration: " I choose to value myself, to treat myself with respect, to declare and fight for my right to exist." This primary act of self-affirmation is the foundation on which self-esteem develops.

Self-acceptance can lie dormant and then suddenly awake. This attitude can fight for our life, even when we are filled with despair. When all we want is to lie down and die, it can impel us to keep moving forward. It is the vital voice of the life force. It is "selfishness," in the highest meaning of that word. If self-acceptance becomes silent, self-esteem is the first casualty.

The second aspect of self-acceptance is our willingness to experience. It is our willingness, without denial or evasion, to honor what we think, what we feel, what we desire, what we have done, and who we are. It is the refusal to regard any part of ourselves as alien. This includes our bodies, our emotions, our thoughts, our actions, and our dreams. Self-acceptance is our willingness to experience rather than disown whatever may be the facts of our being at a particular moment. It is to think our thoughts, own our feelings, and be present to the reality of our behavior.

The third aspect of self-acceptance moves beyond the right to be and the willingness to experience and involves the idea of compassion for self. Suppose I have done something that I regret, or of which I am ashamed, and for which I criticize myself. Self-acceptance does not deny what was done or try to make what was wrong all right. It inquires into the context in which the action was taken. It wishes to understand why something that is wrong or inappropriate felt desirable, appropriate, or even necessary at the time.

I can disapprove of an action I have chosen and still have compassionate interest in the motives that prompted it. I can still choose to be a friend to myself. After I take responsibility for what I have done, I can delve deeper into the context. This kind of accepting, compassionate interest does not encourage unwanted behavior but reduces the likelihood of its recurring.

This self-compassion aspect enables us to criticize or correct ourselves, in ways that do not damage self-esteem. Then we can lead others in the same way. Since future behavior will be shaped by our self-image, we will bring this same benevolence we first give to ourselves to others so we will lead them more effectively. This is the virtue of self-acceptance that is foundational for "true leaders to first lead themselves."

Transformational Leadership, the kind that inspires the greatness of an organization, begins with the leader's own personal transformation. Personal transformation begins with clarity and focus on your identity, purpose, and values. You connect with your highest self when you align them because you create congruency between who you believe you are, what is most important for you to do with your life, and what is most important to you in your life. Your action of alignment is your choice for self-acceptance! When you passionately act upon your identity, purpose, and values through your vision and mission, you will achieve the personal transformational results that you can then apply to your organization as the transformational leader.

As a true leader, you must first lead yourself before you can effectively lead your organization. You begin with the consciousness of who you are and the courage to accept and be that person. Your choice of self-acceptance is an action of self-value and self-commitment that emanates from the reality that you are alive and conscious. As a powerful leader, the development of high self-esteem grows from the seeds of your identity, purpose and values. These seeds are germinated by self-value, cultivated by willingness to experience, and watered by self-compassion, your actions of self-acceptance. Your actions of self-acceptance grow the seeds of your self-esteem.

The experience of low self-esteem is the first obstacle to becoming a highly effective and true leader. This experience is caused by a low self-image that is caused by unconscious negative beliefs about yourself. These beliefs create a weakened mental state and a loss of power, which perpetuates ineffective behaviors towards others and yourself. However, your consistent choices of self-acceptance will create a new life experience of empowerment, which strengthens your mental state and increases your self-esteem. Your self-image becomes positive, optimistic, and strong. Your behaviors change because you become confident in your competence. You mentally shift from conscious competence to unconscious competence because your consistent choices of self-acceptance create consistent experiences of high self-esteem. In other words, your repetitious, conscious choices of self-acceptance create conscious feelings and thoughts of high self-esteem (conscious competence) that eventually become unconscious and automatic (unconscious competence). In turn, these experiences of self-esteem produce confidence in competent and effective choices. These confident choices are the actions that become the habits of highly effective and true leaders.

The second obstacle to becoming a highly effective and true leader is your unconscious negative beliefs about your life experiences. The day of my two traumatic experiences in the desert of Baja California Sur, Mexico, taught me that what I do *not* know can kill me! That is, what I believe unconsciously may affect my choices for actions that could lead to death! I almost lost my life twice on that same day because of my negative belief that I could not trust others with something as important as my life or survival. However, when I saw the face of death before me as I lay in the hot sand of the scorching desert sun and thought: "I'm going to die," I made the ultimate choice of self-acceptance! I also heard the voice of a life force resonating deep from within my soul saying: "I will live!" "I will survive!" The voice impelled me to stand up and keep moving.

My choice for self-acceptance at that moment in the desert was a choice to live because I valued my life; I knew who I was and I knew my purpose in life! While I had the self-esteem to act on self-acceptance to survive in the face of death, I lacked the consciousness to trust another human being to possibly prevent the near-death experiences.

My extraordinary act of self-acceptance propelled me to a new height of self-esteem and consciousness that expanded my awareness of choices in the face of extreme adversity. I became conscious through this ultimate experience of self-acceptance that, if I can first trust and lead myself with something as important as my life or survival, then I could also trust in teamwork with others to survive together in a life-threatening experience.

More likely, your unconscious negative beliefs may affect your choices for action that could figuratively lead to death. There are numerous examples of the results of these choices. Your unconscious negative beliefs may affect your choices that lead to the death of a dream, a personal and/or professional vision and mission, a great idea, a career, a relationship, a team, or even the death of your privately owned or family business.

Whatever your death experience may be, as a result of a choice affected by one of your unconscious negative beliefs, you can change it and prevent it from recurring by accepting yourself for choosing this experience. Your self-acceptance of the experience will increase your self- esteem, which will expand your consciousness or awareness of alternative choices to lead you in a new direction of increased growth and performance. Then, you will be in a strong and powerful state of mind to lead others in your organization.

Your future behaviors or choices of action as a highly effective and true leader are shaped by both your unconscious, low self-image, causing your low self-esteem, as well as your unconscious, negative beliefs about your life experiences. Either can be an obstacle to becoming a true leader. Both obstacles can be overcome by the same solution: The choice to *lead yourself first* by acting on self-acceptance. Lead yourself first, and you will truly inspire and lead the greatness of your organization!

About Dr. Bill Newman

*D*r. *Bill Newman is CEO of Executive Beacon, Inc., an executive development company that works with executive teams and their leaders who want to maximize results in growth and performance. Bill is a consulting psychologist, executive coach, and expert in leadership development who speaks professionally. As a consultant, facilitator and speaker, Bill helps CEOs, presidents, and executives to develop, inspire and lead the greatness of their corporations for the enduring results they want. Bill's customized executive development programs, keynote speeches, and business presentations address leadership, management, peak performance, change, stress, sales, and corporate trust. For over seventeen years, his international programs have been so effective for producing sustained results in corporate growth and performance, he has been featured in* Forbes, Inc., Success, U.S.A. Today, Wall Street Journal, *National Public Radio's "Morning Edition," and CBS TV. Internationally, Bill has appeared in newspapers, radio and television programs in Montreal, Toronto, London, and Paris. Bill is a member of the National Speakers Association and a member of the Board of Directors of the New England Speakers Association.*

Contact Information:
Dr. Bill Newman
Executive Beacon, Inc.
Hamilton Gateway Building
5 Market Square
Suite 101
Amesbury, MA 01913
Phone: 1-800-908-2009
Fax: (978) 834-0990
E-mail: Bill@ExecutiveBeacon.com
Website: www. Executive Beacon.com

Resource Listing

Karen L. Anderson
Anderson Catalyst Training Services (ACTS)
7923 Noland Road
Lenexa, KS 66215-2528
Phone: (913) 492-3881
Fax: (913) 492-5054
E-mail: karen @acts-ion.com
Website: www.acts-ion.com

Dana May Casperson
The Power Etiquette Group
P.O. Box 3637
Santa Rosa, CA 95402
E-mail:
  danamay@PowerEtiquette.com
Website: www.PowerEtiquette.com

Linda Logan-Condon
LTD Unlimited
11728 Linn Avenue NE
Albuquerque, NM 87123
Phone: (505) 292-8015
Fax: (505) 293-5270
E-mail: lloganc@flash.net
Website: www.ltdunlimited.com

Michael Connor
Creative Transitions
8 Nauset Road
Brockton, MA 02301
Phone: (508) 584-9062
Fax: (508) 580-6466
E-mail: MC@ThriveOnChange.com
Website: www.ThriveOnChange.com

Michelle Cubas
Positive Potentials, LLC
7120 E. Sixth Avenue, Suite 21
Scottsdale, AZ 85251
Phone: (480) 922-9699
Fax: (480) 663-6851
E-mail:
  MCubas@PositivePotentials.com
Website: www.PositivePotentials.com

Bonnie Dean
W.O.W. Presentations
4840 Fremont Street
Bellingham, WA 98220
Phone: (800) 915-4668
E-mail: Bonnie@BonnieDean.com
Website: www.bonniedean.com

Jim Lane
Character Vision
607 South Evers Street
Plant City, FL 33563
Phone: (813) 754-5779
Fax: (813) 759-6631
E-mail: Jim@CharacterVision.net
Website: www.CharacterVision.net

Natalie Manor
Natalie Manor & Associates
P.O. Box 1508
Merrimack, NH 03054
Phone: (603) 424-7700
Fax: (603) 424-1267
E-mail:
  CoachNatalie@NatalieManor.com
Website: www.NatalieManor.com

Chet R. Marshall
Elevation Express
130 Summit Ridge
Hurricane, WV 25526
Phone: (304) 545-5100
Fax: (304) 757-5651
E-mail: chetinwv@aol.com

Michele Matt
Inspiring Solutions
2709 Scenic Place
West Des Moines, IA 50265
Phone: (515) 225-1249
Fax: (515) 225-9396
E-mail:
   Michele@InspiringSolutions.com
Website:
   www.InspiringSolutions.com

Dr. Bill Newman
Executive Beacon, Inc.
Hamilton Gateway Building
5 Market Square
Suite 101
Amesbury, MA 01913
Phone: 1-800-908-2009
Fax: (978) 834-0990
E-mail: Bill@ExecutiveBeacon.com
Website: www. Executive Beacon.com

Edie Raether
Performance PLUS
4717 Ridge Water Court
Holly Spring, NC 27540
Phone: (919) 557-7900
Fax: (919) 557-7999
E-mail: edie@raether.com
Website: www.raether.com

Steve Rutledge
Farmers Mutual Hail Insurance Co.
2323 Grand Avenue
Des Moines, IA 50312
Phone: (515) 237-7318
Fax: (515) 237-7397
E-mail: steve@fmh.com

Doug Smart
Smart Business Seminars
P.O. Box 768024
Roswell, GA 30076
Phone: (770) 587-9784
E-mail:Doug@DougSmart.com
Website: www.DougSmart.com

Sharon Spano
Spano & Company, Inc.
649 Stonefield Loop
Heathrow, Florida 32746
Phone: (407) 333-0224
Fax: (407) 444-3840
E-mail: Sharon@SharonSpano.com
Website: www.sharonspano.com

Drew Stevens
Getting to the Finish Line
627 Thorntree Lane
Eureka, St. Louis, MO 63025
Phone: (636) 928-4486
Phone: (toll free) (877) 391-6821
E-mail:
   drew@gettingtothefinishline.com
Website:
   www.gettingtothefinishline.com

Resource Listing

PAGE 255

Dan Thurmon
Motivation Works, Inc.
1905 Scenic Highway,
Suite 640-214
Snellville, GA 30078
Phone: (770) 982-2664
E-mail: dan@danthurmon.com
Website: www.danthurmon.com

Dave Timmons
Extreme Leadership Solutions
P.O. Box 340025
Tampa FL 33694-0025
Phone: (813) 792-9829
Fax: (813) 792-9810
E-mail: Dave@DaveTimmons.com
Website: www.DaveTimmons.com

Jim Vance
Advanced Business Resources
4912 Yoakum Boulevard
Houston, TX 77006
Phone: (713) 527-8893
E-mail: jim@abr-training.com
Website: www.abr-training.com

Susan Wilson
Executive Strategies, Inc.
1105 W. 12th Street South
Newton, IA 50208
Phone: (641) 791-7904
E-mail: susan@execstrategies.com
Website: www.execstrategies.com

Candy Whirley
SBG Services, LLC
4409 NE 48th Terrace
Kansas City, MO 64119
Phone: (816) 455-4753
Fax: (816) 455-4753
E-mail: cwhirley@kc.rr.com